John was born in Aveley, Essex and was educated at his local comprehensive. After leaving school, he worked as a mechanical engineer, before making the transition to civil engineering. John is married, with a son and daughter, and is now retired which has given him the opportunity to fulfil a longstanding ambition to write a novel about a young London highwayman from the late 18th century, which he felt was a story that had to be shared.

Dedicated to my father, Robert Kinnear Rigby.

J P Rigby

DAMN YOUR EYES...STOP!

The Story of London Highwayman
Lewis Jeremiah Avershaw

AUSTIN MACAULEY PUBLISHERS™

LONDON * CAMBRIDGE * NEW YORK * SHARJAH

A CIP catalogue record for this title is available from the British Library.

ISBN 9781398430983 (Paperback)
ISBN 9781398430990 (ePub e-book)

www.austinmacauley.com

First Published 2022
Austin Macauley Publishers Ltd®
1 Canada Square
Canary Wharf
London
E14 5AA

Thanks to Ivan Butler and also More Visual Ltd, for their artistic support.

Take Heed

As I swing in the wind
I watch ye
Even though I have no eyes

Ye come in droves
To view me
Now ye know
Why I despise

A curse I lay upon ye
Unaware it has been passed

Smile and stare hyenas
Your joy it will not last!

Southwark, London, England 1782

THE SMALL, solitary figure of a young boy lingered impatiently on the gloomy rain-soaked steps of St Saviour's Parochial School. The day had just ended, and the children were making their way home as quickly as possible. The chilling, stench-ridden air chased through the damp, open streets and alleyways from the smoggy river's edge…not the best of days for loitering. Speeding home as quickly as possible and warming themselves next to a welcoming open fire was what ran through most of the children's minds, but not that of young Lewis Jeremiah Avershaw, known as Jerry to his family and friends.

He was awaiting the appearance of his friends. There were things to discuss, things to be done and plans to be made for the evening ahead. They were the original latchkey children and making a little bit of money by whatever means possible was right there at the top of their agenda.

A slightly built, dark-haired boy of much the same ilk swaggered over to him, accompanied by two others. He was born to the name of Henry Watts. The four boys, on first impression, couldn't be mistaken for anything other than what they were – trouble.

Whenever there was a minor incident in the school yard, or anywhere else for that matter, nine times out of ten they were right there, deep in the thick of it. Even in these early stages of their young lives, their intentions to make a mark as young men not to be messed with came across loud and very, very clear. Intimidation and the taking of food and money or anything else that came to hand was a regular everyday occurrence that younger and weaker children had to endure, knowing that if they told a soul, there would be severe repercussions to follow.

For minds so young, the four boys understood all too well the workings of fear, the human thought process and circumstance, not to mention their own social standing in life, where an obsession with diverting themselves from the same path in life as that of their fathers and brothers was clear enough proof to try something different.

'Keep nicking as much as you can and improve your quality of life. Nice clothes, look like a dandy young gent and impress the girls.'

This was all that mattered to the young thieves and nothing was going to stop them reaching their destination.

As they gathered together, whispers were exchanged and plans were made to rendezvous that evening before dispersing in opposite directions back to their dismal tenements.

As Jerry arrived home and entered the front door, he instinctively knew that something was wrong – it was too quiet. He called through to his mother, who appeared at the top of the stairs, and before she could utter a single word, he asked her what was going on.

'It's your father, he's had an accident at work and has injured his back. He's lying on the floor next to his bed. It's the only place that's comfortable for him.'

Jerry's father was a labourer at the dye works on Bankside. He knew his father was always hauling and lifting heavy crates day in, day out, and suffered recurrent "twinges" of pain down his left leg, to his toes. He would say that his lower back was "giving him grief" as he tried his best to undermine the seriousness of his ever-recurring problem when he tried to pull himself out of his chair. It would take him a few moments to "loosen up" before he could straighten himself. It looked as if this was the final straw that had broken the camel's back.

Jerry climbed the stairs anxiously, looking into his parents' room. As he did so his heart skipped a beat. He was disturbed by what he saw. His father gave him a coy smile, but Jerry knew that he was putting on a brave front for him. Jerry remembered his father once telling him, 'If you want to know if someone is telling you the truth, look deep into their eyes. They're the windows to the brain, and they'll tell you exactly what they're thinking.' When Jerry did that to his father, he could see a hard-working, good man suffering and not knowing when he would be able to earn a wage again. Hard physical graft had destroyed his body.

He sat and talked to his father for a short time, until his mother called him for his evening meal. As he toyed with his food, he looked at his mother.

'How are we going to get by with Father out of work?' he asked inquisitively.

'Don't worry, darling,' came the reply. 'I'll have to take on some more washing from the inns down the road, but we'll get by.'

Jerry knew things were going to be tight until his father could get back on his feet but decided to go along with his mother's words. He didn't see any point in scratching at an open wound. And besides, he knew it wouldn't be long before he took employment with the innkeeper who ran the post-chaise service down the road, who had promised his father that he would give Jerry a start. He was looking forward to earning some decent money.

After he'd eaten, Jerry headed off out to meet his friends, much to his mother's dismay.

'They'll get you in trouble again, you mark my words,' she told him, referring to some previous bother he'd got himself into with them some weeks earlier. She knew it was only a matter of time before he would end up in front of the judge again, and next time his leniency wouldn't be so generous. 'Keep away from them, do you hear me, Jerry Avershaw? They're no good. You keep hanging around with them and you'll end up dying with your boots on, you mark my words.'

His mother's reference to being hanged and her desperate pleas fell upon deaf ears.

******

As Jerry approached the small benched area next to Blackfriars Bridge, he could see that his friends were already there, talking amongst themselves and waiting for his appearance. They had had some previous success as pickpockets but had almost got their comeuppance when they were spotted by a lady who was window shopping nearby. Fortunately for them they had managed to make their escape without any reprisals, but it had been enough to scare them into venting their criminal ways into a different direction. Well, for a short time at least, until things cooled a little and they regained their self-confidence.

In the past they would break into the dockside huts and small lock-ups that were scattered along the banks of the Thames, but the old watchman became familiar with their ways and the previous victims of their crimes had also made their properties harder to break into.

This time they had decided to "look over" properties on the other side of the water, in the hope of finding a suitable house where they would take what they could there and then. The boys worked well as a team, with the youngest used as look-outs, while the older and braver boys would knock the door first and run away sharpish. If someone came to the door, chances are they would think it was only scallywags playing games. If, on the other hand, nobody answered, then further investigation would be made.

The more they got away with, the more brazen they became. Food would be taken, even the odd rabbit didn't escape their clutches. Jewellery, boots, clothes and, of course, money – anything of value.

They took their food home, often with a lame excuse for how it had been acquired, and everything else was "fenced" to big George Alston, or a local innkeeper who knew George, and was located close by their school. As time passed, the boys left school and found themselves work of one kind or another.

******

The innkeeper friend of Jerry's father was true to his word and gave Jerry employment, training him for the position of a post-chaise driver. Jerry learned fast and, upon making the grade, secured a permanent position within the company, although this didn't dampen his enthusiastic spirits for his little hobby of house-breaking.

He and his gang enjoyed their new world, earning a daily wage and supplementing it with the proceeds of their criminal activities. They began to buy clothes that lifted their spirits and made them feel good about themselves. Nobody seemed to look down on them anymore as they frequented places of public amusement within the neighbourhood of St George's Fields, looking very distinguished with their extravagant style of dress and profuse expenditure.

It wasn't long before they began to associate with the respectable young gentlemen of the area, who were unaware of their backgrounds. However, after a while, it became more apparent that the gentlemen were associating with young men of the type best avoided. After a few drinks, the boys soon fell into their usual familiar ways, their tongues became looser and their true natures became exposed. Their new-found friends made themselves scarce, drifting away to socialise elsewhere and avoiding the unsavoury characters who dared to invade their social lifestyle.

While the boys' social standing took a turn for the worse amongst the middle and upper classes, elsewhere money still talked louder than words and none more so than amongst the courtesans of St George's Fields. If you could maintain an air of respectability for as long as you were in their company and reward them no differently to those of the upper classes, then that would do just fine.

Jerry Avershaw would visit one such pretty lady, Nancy Abram, and visit her often he did. It was at this time that Jerry took it upon himself to leave home and take lodgings at a country inn by the name of the Bald Faced Stag, which perched solitarily by the edge of the road in Putney Vale.

He still pursued his honest work for the hackney carriage company, but times were changing. The young, well-dressed man who was made welcome at the inn carried with him a dark side, yet to be discovered, and it was soon to be accelerated by his good friend Henry Watts, who was about to join him and take a room there too.

The Red Lion Tavern,
St George's Fields, London
3 December 1790

LOOK, IT'S him again,' said Henry in no more than a faint whisper. Jerry didn't utter a word in reply to his friend but just stared in dumbfounded fascination at the man's cocky and extrovert mannerisms as he called to the tavern keeper for ale and wine to satisfy his entourage of worshippers.

They had noticed him earlier in the day outside a coffee house, mounted on as fine a stallion as one could acquire, tipping his gold-braided hat at a pretty young girl who happened to pass close by. They couldn't hear what he'd said to her, but it made her blush profusely and smile, so she was obviously flattered by his unexpected comments.

'Don't you know who that is boys?' said a small, frail old man, sitting in the corner close by, who had been watching them with interest.

'No. Do you?' asked Jerry, unable to take his eyes off the cocksure character.

'That's Black Jack. John James the highwayman. You must have heard of him,' said the old man, as he clambered from his chair, retrieving his walking stick and pointing it disrespectfully in the highwayman's direction. 'Keep away from that one. He has two personalities, and you're looking at the better one,' he mumbled scornfully, as he brushed past them and made his way to the door.

The bold, brazen highwayman's chances of one day meeting with the hangman were good, but it didn't seem to bother him one jot. For Jerry and Henry, this man's total disregard of law and order and the fact that he'd been getting away with his crimes without the Bow Street Runners feeling his collar was more than enough to take their own criminal activities to a higher level.

Putney Heath, London
Eight Days Later, 6.30 am

A LARGE carriage appeared in the distance, moving at a good speed, only slowing as it approached the junction. Two masked horsemen, heavily armed, moved swiftly from the dense copse on to the dusty, hard, compacted road. Speed was everything.

'Damn your eyes…Stop!' Ordered one of the highwaymen, his flintlock pointing menacingly towards the face of the coachman. 'I mean what I say, fucker!'

The coachman reluctantly took heed of the man's words, but his mind was thinking differently. His hand began to twitch nervously as he considered his chances of reaching for his blunderbuss. However, the darkly dressed figure opposing him was aware of his intentions, and his unconcealable hostility caused the coachman to take stock and recoil back from the weapon.

The masked gunman picked up the blunderbuss and glanced over it, his dark brown eyes closing to near slits as he read the engraved words that ran along its barrel. 'Fly or die,' said the highwayman scornfully, laughing sarcastically.

The coachman's face paled with the instant realisation that events were about to get worse, as the highwayman's mask failed to conceal the evil grin that lay beneath. The masked man's dilated eyes widened, piercing with belligerence and hatred as he locked on to those of his victim.

'I choose to do neither! But you'll die if you don't do as you're fucking told,' the highwayman said.

He was Jerry Avershaw, and his accomplice, Henry Watts, positioned himself by the carriage door, beckoning its three occupants, two men and one woman, to join him outside in the cool morning elements.

'Good morning, gents! And how are you my lovely?' said Henry caustically, as he sped up the older of the two men with a shove. 'Remove your coats!' He added with an authoritative growl.

The men's pockets were searched. Both were packing pocket pistols. Henry checked the makers' names quickly whilst keeping a watchful eye on his prey. 'Bass, London,' he mused. 'A very good maker.' He was happy, and he placed the pistols into his sack.

'Now remove your boots!' Jerry ordered. The older of the two men again dithered, so Henry rushed towards him, anger oozing out of every pore of his body, knocking the old man's hat to the ground as he descended upon him, and forcing the barrel of his pistol deep into his chest.

'Remove your fucking boots!' Henry yelled with frustration.

The old man's floundering efforts bordered on the theatrical as he struggled to lift his leg and rolled backwards like an upturned beetle. Jerry's hostility turned to uncontrollable laughter, giggling close to tears as the old man tried his utmost to please his persecutors. He fumbled and rolled around in vain, desperately trying to remove his boots. He eventually reached his moment of success, and in doing so a purse fell from each boot to the ground almost simultaneously.

Jerry's laughter accelerated. 'Humpty Dumpty, you sly old fox! You just can't trust anyone these days.' His attention suddenly turned upon the shivering, frightened young woman.

'Remove your necklace and rings,' Jerry ordered, and took them from the woman, placing them into his sack. The young woman had complied without the slightest hint of hatred or contempt in her eyes.

'Please, hand me your purse,' Jerry asked her, his tone mellowing considerably. The young woman looked at him with a timid curiosity as she relinquished her purse. Jerry's eyes warmed as he looked at her. She had a glow of innocence in her pale blue eyes that he'd never encountered before.

He opened the purse and peered inside. It contained a small silver vinaigrette and two guinea pieces. He closed the purse and handed it back to her. She gave him a glimpse of a smile.

'Thank you,' she whispered. She spoke with a calm mellow restraint, unlike the familiar patronising gravelly edged tones that Jerry had grown so accustomed to. Frustration raced through his body, knowing he would never encounter a woman of her type on a romantic level.

Henry climbed into the carriage while Jerry held the coachman and its passengers at gunpoint. He emerged moments later with two silver tankards and a bottle of good stock brandy.

'Leave them,' said Jerry, in an unfamiliar act of kindness.

Henry placed the items back inside the carriage, murmuring under his breath, 'All over a pretty one.'

The two highwaymen climbed back on to their horses and took their leave. The coachman's face flushed red with rage as the high tobys galloped away into the distance. He rained heavy blows of frustration upon his carriage's immaculate coachwork. 'One day those scamps will meet with the rope, and the sooner the bloody better,' he said.

'Quite possibly, coachman,' said the younger of his male passengers, 'but can we now make our way back to some kind of security. I'm sure we all feel quite vulnerable out here, and besides, this has to be reported immediately.'

The Green Man Inn, Putney Heath
That Evening

JERRY AVERSHAW and Henry Watts edged their way through the crowded alehouse. A powerfully built man, tall in stature, beckoned them over to join him and his three smartly dressed companions. Outwardly, they gave the impression of London gents, but that was where the similarity ended. Their harsh accents and aloof manner towards strangers were all tell-tale signs that they had graduated from the school of hard knocks.

The big man selectively homed in on one of the barmaids and gestured for two more ales for his friends. She acknowledged him with a nod and a smile, pouring their drinks and bringing them over. It was evident that the big man and the barmaid were very fond of each other.

'Anything else, George?' she asked in a mild, well-spoken northern accent.

'No, Jenny. We're fine for now. Thanks love,' the big man replied with a boyish smile, out of keeping with his usual rhetoric.

One of the big man's companions, Thomas Ledbury, was observing George and Jenny, then he directed his gaze towards Jerry and Henry. He nodded his head and pointed towards big George, whilst raising his eyebrows and grinning, mocking the lovebirds in a schoolboy manner.

George ignored Thomas, addressing his new guests. 'I've ordered a shoulder of mutton to be roasted for our supper. I hope you two are going to join us for the evening.' Jerry and Henry accepted his offer and discussed their day with the others. All six of them were in high spirits.

George was the eldest of the men, who had a history between them that went back further than one would expect. George was also the man who had fenced Jerry's and Henry's stolen goods back in their schooldays and had "educated" them in their criminal apprenticeships. He'd gathered a priceless knowledge of the London underworld, which he'd shared with his young protégés.

He looked older than his thirty-four years, possibly due to his incarceration on the prison hulk *Censor*. Some said he was fortunate not to have been transported. A permanent reminder of this period of his life was carried in the form of a deep scar that ran vertically down the left side of his face, narrowly missing his eye, received after an ugly brawl with three of the prison guards.

As the evening progressed and the ale flowed more than it should have, George told them of a story he'd read in the newspaper earlier in the day. It had caught his eye as it was something that he would never have thought about in such a situation. He went on to tell of a gentleman and his dog, a big mastiff, walking over the heath, when they were stopped by a footpad near the Hounslow turnpike. The footpad demanded the man's purse, not seeing the dog, which had wandered off amongst the bushes. The man gave a whistle and an order to the animal, which had been trained as a guard dog. It attacked the footpad ferociously, biting him in several places, some of which were worse than others. The dog, at his master's word, then guarded the fellow until he was handed over to the watch.

George paused for a moment. 'Always be ready for the unexpected, heh!' he remarked, whilst downing the remains of his ale.

Henry looked at George, then said, 'The footpad was obviously a jester. You simply shoot the beast and let the fucker know in no uncertain terms that he'll get the same unless he hands over.'

George's friend James Myers looked at Henry, po-faced. 'Maybe that's where the footpad went wrong. He probably only had a fruit knife,' James quipped.

They all broke out into laughter and George wagged his finger at his friend. 'Good point, good point.' He chuckled.

The Sword Blade Coffee House
Birching Lane, London
16 January 1791, 10 am

JERRY, HENRY and James Myers sat tentatively, cupping their hot coffees in their hands, trying their utmost to nurse their self-inflicted wounds from the night before. They watched as the large dark oak door of the coffee house opened and their three fellow sufferers shuffled in gingerly. George Alston and Thomas Ledbury were followed by a very nauseated and pale-looking Ned Simpson.

'I've seen corpses with more colour in their faces!' said Jerry, with a ridiculing grin, causing Henry to crack a forced smile.

'Fuck off,' mumbled Ned Simpson, aware that the mocking remark was directed at himself rather than anyone else. Ned had known Jerry and Henry since childhood, when he wasn't one of the happiest of kids.

As a small boy he was sold for the paltry sum of one guinea by his family because they couldn't afford to keep him. Fortunately, he was reasonably well looked after by his adoptive parents, although the scars of hurt ran deep inside him. He could never understand why his parents had abandoned him like they did, no matter how poor they were. He'd confided in Jerry one day when they were two ten-year-olds sitting along the banks of the Thames, that he believed he was bought specifically to be used as a lackey. The local children used to call him by the name of Jack Hall, after the infamous villain whose parents sold him for just one guinea to be used as a climbing boy whilst only a child. Jack Hall had become bitter towards the harsh world in which he lived and became a rebellious tearaway. When he was about to be hanged at Tyburn in 1707, he unleashed the inelegant curse, 'Damn your eyes,' at the people he held so much hatred towards.

Ned could feel Jack Hall's pain. He shared something with him that he wouldn't wish on his worst enemy. Ned stood around five feet ten inches tall, and was fair-haired and slim with broad powerful shoulders, much like George Alston. His handsome rugged face could easily be mistaken for that of a pugilist, for he carried the characteristic battle-damaged nose of a young man who had seen more than his fair share of bar room brawls, although this didn't seem to be a factor that deterred the ladies, much to Jerry's amusement. When they rode through the busy London streets on their jet-black mares, Jerry couldn't help but notice the admiring glances the ladies gave Ned.

'Listen!' said George abruptly. 'I have something to tell you. I've been given some worthwhile information from the ostler at the Bull and Swan. There are three well-heeled gambling men staying under his roof for the night and they're making their way down to Wrotham in Kent for the big fight between Johnson and Bryan the day after tomorrow. Apparently, they're big gamblers and will be carrying large sums of money. The ostler had quite a chat with one of them and was told that the Duke of Hamilton was supplying Bryan's stake to fight Johnson for a prize of five hundred guineas. Also, the ostler overheard him talking to the coachman, a man by the name of Tilby. I know of the man, a big surly fucker. I knew his brother. A right sarcastic little bastard he was too.'

'Isn't he around anymore then?' asked Ned, curious. 'No, no, he's not around anymore. They found him slumped in his dirty old chair, in his dirty little house, his supper still in his lap, dead as a dodo he was. He was only forty, never had a wife or anything like that. As I said, nobody cared for him much.' George laughed to himself. 'It sounds like even his own body had had enough of him.'

'What did the ostler have to say, George?' asked Henry dryly, trying to direct his friend back on track with the conversation.

'Oh yeh,' George continued. 'Apparently they'll be heavily armed and Tilby apparently has been tipped generously to be extra vigilant.'

'What time do they set off?' asked Jerry.

'Four o'clock in the afternoon, but they're picking up a friend in Putney on the way. Apparently, he couldn't be with them because he had some work to finish, so they'll be on the road around a quarter before five. That's how the ostler sees it.'

Jerry nodded with a smile of approval. He'd known "Yorkshire Jack" the ostler for some time and carried great respect for his knowledge and capabilities around people and horses. He could also estimate journey times with an uncanny accuracy, something the wise old man had acquired over years of observation.

Jack had been a valuable asset to George over the years, and also shared many a barnstorming drinking session with him. They enjoyed each other's company and shared the same humour, and of course Jack enjoyed all the free ale that came his way, something he wasn't going to turn his nose up at. Big George also paid him handsomely for his information, which always ended in a good earner.

Jack's information always resulted in an abundance of riches that was way beyond that of a normal outing for Jerry, which meant he could halve his outings and, of course, halve his chances of getting caught. It was, as George put it, "a marriage made in heaven". It was also good for Jack's retirement fund, which if not for their little agreement would be practically non-existent.

Putney Common, London
16 January 1791, 4.45 pm

A HEAVILY laden carriage thundered over the horizon, making its way towards the turnpike. As it slowed to a stop, the guard's cussing yells of disapproval rang out as he shooed away the tinkers pestering the men within. The coachman hastily paid the gatekeeper his toll and the gate was lifted with vigour, allowing the carriage to continue on its way down the long straight road at breakneck speed. It threw up blustering clouds of sandy dust in its wake, everyone oblivious to the steely-eyed silhouetted figures monitoring their every move as they approached the point of interception.

Tilby the coachman instinctively cracked his whip, pushing his heavily perspiring horses beyond their comfort zone as they thundered towards the dense woodland, aware of the imposing dangers that could be lurking within. The high tobymen expected nothing less from the experienced coachman, who was unknowingly playing right into their conniving, manipulating hands.

'What the hell! Boulders. Boulders in the road!' yelled the guard hysterically as Tilby raised himself from his seat, pulling on the reins with every ounce of strength his body could muster. The carriage twisted, juddered and swerved violently as it tried desperately to change its course away from the impending threat that lay in its path, before plummeting into the rough terrain of the common and grinding to an abrupt shuddering holt.

The panic-stricken passengers peered nervously out of their windows, only to witness their worst fears unfolding before their very eyes as they caught sight of the fast-flitting figures of the highwaymen descending upon them from within the shadows of the woods.

A ball was fired over the top of the stricken carriage, sending its horses into a further skittish frenzy and dragging the carriage unceremoniously deeper into the common's hazardous terrain. It forced the guard and coachmen to abandon their seats for the safety of the ground.

'Raise your hands high, coachman. Now!' One of the highwaymen demanded. The big disgruntled coachman returned a cold hard stare at the highwayman, no compliance given. 'Damn your fucking eyes, coachman! Do as you're fucking told, or I swear I'll be done with you!' The coachman's face flushed with rage as he submitted to reluctant obedience.

BANG! A shot from another high toby's pistol strayed from its barrel, its echo reverberating throughout the woodland like a Chinese firecracker on New Year's Day. The guard dropped heavily to the ground, grasping desperately at the torn, blood-soaked flesh that hung grotesquely from his incapacitated leg, his foolhardy bravery repaid at high cost.

'Move away from that blunderbuss. I won't ask twice!' growled George Alston, his deep rasping voice tinged with psychotic vindictiveness at the man's sheer audacity in taking such a liberty.

Thomas Ledbury and James Myers remained mounted on their horses, their pistols trained through the carriage windows at the four gambling men seated within.

'Good afternoon, gentlemen. Kindly disembark slowly and with great caution and maintain a dignified reserve if you please!' said James Myers with a sarcastic benevolent grin noticeably apparent beneath his mask.

The four men complied with his flippant demand, only to be greeted with a vision that made their hearts sink to the lowest of depths. Tilby the coachman had been forced to kneel on the ground, the barrel of Jerry Avershaw's pistol embedded deep into his mouth with despicable contempt, chipping his front teeth.

Meanwhile, Henry Watts systematically sifted through the men's pockets, liberating a handsome gold card case containing one of the men's business cards. He looked over it and smiled under his mask.

'So, you're a London tea trader,' Henry remarked.

'Yes, that's correct,' came the short reluctant reply.

'Well, you don't know who we are, but we know who you are, so if you get any little urges to pursue us, you might find it in your best interest to fight them, because you'll be placing not only yourselves but your families at risk. Do you understand where I'm coming from?' warned Henry. The men expressed their acknowledgment with restrained nods.

'Well, well. What have we here then?' came an excited cry from within the carriage. It was James Myers, whose over-zealous words of surprise would have made the most passionate of actors proud of their performance as he and Thomas Ledbury hauled out a heavy strongbox from under the passengers' seat. The four passengers looked on despondently.

'Keys please, gents!' said James Myers, concealing yet another smile under his mask. The box was opened. Thomas Ledbury instantly transferred the money into his sack.

'And where were you going with such a grand sum of money? You. Yes, you!' said James Myers, pointing his pistol in the direction of one of the men. 'You tell me!'

'We are, or should I say were, on our way to see the Johnson – Bryan fight for the championship of England. The money was our stake money,' the man replied.

'My, my, you must be top-drawer gamblers or very good businessmen to risk such large sums of money. Which is it?' asked James.

'Bit of both I suppose,' replied the man, choosing his words carefully in the hope not to displease.

'Well, I tip my hat to yah boys. At least you're not some inherited wealth, spoilt brats, who fritter it away without any understanding of its true value!' said James, as he glanced over to Jerry.

'So, you're gambling men?' asked Jerry, as he continued his menacing stance over the coachman.

'Yes, yes, we are,' one of the passengers replied.

'Well, here's a bet you can be bloody sure of,' Jerry continued. 'We'll be taking your money and gone within two minutes, and if you don't turn in your tracks and return to where you came from, things will get worse for you!'

The high tobymen were true to their word. Within two minutes they were gone, melting into the distant woodland, leaving their victims to solemnly make their way back to the toll gate.

The Nags Head, Princes Street, Drury Lane, London
8 March 1791, 8 pm

JERRY AND Henry were sitting with Ned Simpson in an alcove, drinking and waiting for the arrival of George.

There was some business to attend to with him before they set off to meet the ladies at St George's Fields.

They often met here. It had been a regular haunt of George's for several years. He'd known the previous landlord, Jack Grimes, well until it changed hands just over a year or so ago. Jack was known to every thief and vagabond as "lawyer Grimes", and to his close friends simply as "the lawyer", a title that stuck after he managed to evade the clutches of the law when they attempted to charge him with receiving stolen goods that were discovered on his premises. He'd discovered a flaw in the prosecution's evidence and exploited it to the full to regain his freedom on a technicality.

George often fenced his goods to "the lawyer", but after that little scare decided to move all of his ill-gotten stock through the safe hands of a mutual close friend by the name of Wolf. Indeed, Wolf and "the lawyer" were a closely connected duo within London's dark side of capital operators and manipulators. George would often joke that the pair of them had the skills and influence to shift a herd of elephants between them, without the slightest inkling of suspicion being aroused, but that optimistic theory was soon to be dispersed when Grimes's luck took a turn for the worse.

The authorities didn't take kindly to being made into a laughing stock, and discreetly set about watching Grimes's activities from afar, eventually bringing him to justice on a charge of receiving a large quantity of fish that was known to have been stolen. This time there were no discrepancies in the evidence to exploit. The judge, with tongue in cheek and an air of great satisfaction and smugness, told him: 'This time, Mr Grimes, you have been reeled in without any chance of getting off the hook.'

Lawyer Grimes had no choice but to accept his fishy fate and was duly transported for seven years. These days, things had changed, and it was a place where good company met, especially in the evenings. Each man would call for his own half pint of wine or a gill if he pleased.

Although the house furnished no supper, each evening a woman attended with mutton pies, which had become very popular. As Jerry, Henry and Ned sat quietly, their attention was drawn to two elegantly dressed women making their way through the busy house towards a table occupied by a couple nearby. They were closely followed by two smartly dressed men who were clearly in their company. They all greeted one another, and the newcomers sat down with the others within earshot of the high tobys.

As their conversation unfolded, it became evident that the man who took centre stage in the conversation was a reputable surgeon. He spoke with an air of authority as if he were addressing students at his medical school. Henry found his tone nauseating as they sat listening to him address his captive audience. His non-stop grumbles then turned to a conversation he'd held with a postilion earlier in the day, about a disturbing highway robbery of four gents a month before.

The high tobys' curiosity rose considerably as they listened in on the conversation. The surgeon made it known that it was he who had removed the shot from the guard's leg and that he believed the poor man to have been very fortunate that it wasn't a far more serious outcome for him. He also believed that the four gents weren't alone in their abundant loss, for the guard and poor coachman had a far more daunting mountain to climb than that of financial earnings alone. These poor souls had to return to their livelihoods with the ever-present psychological burden hanging over them that they had a more than reasonable chance of encountering these lowlifes again sometime further down the line if they weren't apprehended.

As the high tobys sat intently listening, the surgeon continued: 'And from what I've read in the newspapers, these men are becoming more and more brazen with every day that passes. I personally blame the government for being so weak. They should take away the licences of every public house that curries favour with these villains, cut down the rookeries and police the shadowy avenues where they lie in wait in order to set upon our honest hard-working citizens who are going about their business.

'But above all we need a good mounted police force to ride after these deplorable thugs. There simply aren't enough good men out there to drag them by the scruff of their necks to the nearest clink until the time comes for them to be properly dealt with by the powers that be. Instead, the government repeals our well-established laws at every God-given opportunity by giving out fresh licences every day to their public houses and saying how awful our picturesque countryside would look if we did such barbaric deeds as chop down our rookeries and thickets. It's enough to make the most restrained of people seethe with anger. I only wish that just half the power that lay in their hands, lay in mine, for make no mistake, if it were down to me, these individuals would be given short shrift!'

Jerry Avershaw looked over at the doctor who was preaching from behind his wine glass and applauded him with slow loud claps. 'Forgive me for intruding upon you, sir,' Jerry said, 'but I couldn't help but overhear your conversation, and I congratulate you on your sincere thoughts on apprehending these scoundrels. I had the misfortune of falling prey to a highwayman myself and it's a life-changing experience, and not for the better, I can tell you!'

'Did you indeed, sir,' the surgeon replied. 'I do hope you didn't come to any physical harm.'

'No, sir, just relieved of my earnings and my pride,' said Jerry with a sigh.

'Well, thank God you came away from your hideous ordeal in good health, sir,' replied the surgeon, hoping to terminate the conversation with the overbearing stranger as quickly as possible.

They all then turned and went about their business, talking amongst themselves at their tables.

'So, where did you get robbed of your pride and money? This is news to me,' asked Ned with a look of apprehension. 'When I played cards with you yesterday,' said Jerry coyly, as he sipped his wine.

'Funny, very funny.' Ned was still grinning as the door opened and in walked George.

'I've shifted all of the weapons and watches. Everything's gone. I'll bring all of the money to Jerry's tomorrow,' George whispered.

'That's good news, George,' replied Jerry.

'I'm not going to make myself comfortable.' Added George. 'I'm going to the Green Man with Thomas and James. See you tomorrow morning at ten o'clock sharp.'

The Bald-Faced Stag Inn, Putney Vale, London
9 March 1791, 10 am

'MORNING, RALPH,' said George Alston as he passed the reins of his horse over into the safe hands of his friend before removing a weather-beaten bag attached to his saddle.

'They're all in there, George, sitting by the window like little skittles as usual, waiting for you,' Ralph replied.

'I know, I saw them as I passed, sitting there looking fragile and hungover. They can't carry on like this. Something's got to give.'

Ralph chuckled. 'For sure, for sure,' he muttered in agreement.

George entered the inn, bag in hand. The men climbed from their chairs and followed him into the back room, closing the door behind them.

George was in high spirits. Life was treating him reasonably well at the moment. The outlaws sat down as George placed his leather bag on the table and removed the money from within. It had already been counted and placed into smaller bags. Each man picked one up and opened it, counting their share. Nobody studied anyone else's to see if they had more because they trusted one another implicitly. It was the glue that kept them together.

They looked at one another fondly, pleased with their spoils, knowing they would all be comfortable for some time to come. A coachman on top wage would have to work excessively for a long, long time to earn such a sum.

Big George looked around and cracked a smile as broad as his shoulders. He was pleased that his friends were happy, so he decided it was a good time to tell them of the other thing he had on his mind. He was after an even bigger payday to turn his dream of owning a tavern with his Jenny into a reality, and the opportunity had placed itself on his doorstep the evening before when he'd been speaking to his brother Samuel, and what passed between Samuel's lips was too tempting a proposal for the ageing desperado.

Big George told his fellow felons of the trip his brother had just made for his employer, Manton & Rigby the gunsmiths, to some gentry by the name of Stokes in Cobham, Surrey. Samuel had been struck by the beauty of the place and the vastness of its stunning, rambling grounds. He also remarked to George about how vulnerable the property looked and its considerable distance from any other habitation. Even his work colleague who made the journey with him couldn't help but notice the property's vulnerability, given that it had so many riches within.

Samuel had also mentioned how someone with bad intentions could easily take advantage of the household without any interference from the Runners or anybody else. Nobody would be able to do anything about it, Samuel believed, which is why they were buying the guns. The rifles were for hunting and the pistols for protection.

'That was when I decided to go down and take a look for myself this morning. I only returned an hour ago,' said George.

'So that's why you smell worse than your horse,' quipped Henry.

'Sharp. Very sharp,' retorted George. 'I'll tell you this. If you come in on this one, we'll all end up smelling of roses, you mark my words!'

'You're pleased with what you saw down there are you George?' asked Henry.

'This is prime for us, believe me,' George replied.

Jerry raised his eyebrows and nodded. 'Then maybe we should all take a ride out there tomorrow and look for ourselves,' he suggested.

'Good, good. Tomorrow it is,' agreed George with a contented smile.

The Bald-Faced Stag Inn, Putney Vale
10 March 1791, 6 am

THE MORNING seemed to have come around quicker than usual. The bleary-eyed outlaws mounted their horses, mesmerised by George's high spirits and abundant supply of energy at such an early time of day.

Henry looked wide-eyed at Jerry in astonishment and said, 'George doesn't need a bloody horse. He could run there on foot, and then wrestle a bear at the end of it. Look at him. Just look at him!'

Jerry laughed. 'I know. I don't know where he gets it from, but I have a feeling we're going to cover these fifteen miles or so in more than good time.'

As the journey progressed, James Myers looked at George. He'd just spotted a building far off in the distance. 'I've passed here before, George. That's the Old Bear Inn,' James said.

'Are you sure?' asked George, with an element of surprise.

'Aye. I passed it about a year ago in my travels. It's a busy little inn,' said James.

'Busy you say. That's good,' George replied. 'I noticed it yesterday but didn't stop. We can rest here before we check over Stokes's place.'

Jerry trotted behind, locked in his own little world. His eyes flitting over his surroundings as he approached the well-kept inn, with the caution of a vixen crossing an open field with its cubs.

The men dismounted and made their way inside. Jerry remained on his horse. Thomas Ledbury gave him a frustrated look and said, 'Aw no. Not a hole?'

Jerry grinned as he replied, 'I know it's a chore, but someone's got to do it.'

'I'm aware of that, but why me?' Thomas grumbled as he climbed back on to his horse.

'Why me? Why me?' mocked Jerry in a high-pitched squeaky voice as they back-tracked down the lane to a location that Jerry had instinctively selected earlier.

Five and thirty minutes slowly ticked by before the two men returned, placing themselves down in front of their ales.

'This Stokes feller… do you think he'll be at home?' asked Jerry.

'Probably,' replied George. 'You know these people. They're all landlords and manipulators. They just take rent for this and rent for that and sit back on their big fat arses, working out who to exploit next. And if they're not doing that all day long, they're banging one of the maids or they're off to the next flat race meeting at Ascot.'

'Aye, that's what makes me so up for this one,' snarled Ned Simpson. 'I know these people haven't worked hard for all their wealth. It's all been handed down on a silver platter, so what we take today will be a drop in the ocean to them. They'll recover from it.'

Jerry nodded in agreement. 'You're right. These people are used to being in control. Do this, do that. And if anyone falls out of favour, they simply have them kicked down the road by one of their minions without having to encounter any confrontation. Today will be the day the boot is on the other foot!'

Jerry noticed that Henry was sitting deep in thought. 'What's up, Henry?' he asked with a beleaguered look.

'Your words remind me of a story my father once told me,' Henry replied. 'When he was working for a stone mason in Blackfriars. There was a young boy who worked there who had three of his fingers missing on his right hand, incurred from an accident he had there a couple of months earlier. The poor lad continued to work the best he could, although his hand was still heavily bandaged. My father told me the bastards ran him ragged and paid him fuck all. One day the poor hungry little devil picked up a pie that had fallen to the ground and rolled in the dirt outside the butcher's shop, thinking it couldn't be sold. He picked it up, dusted it off and set about eating it. Well, he only took one bite from it before they grabbed him and flogged him mercilessly to within an inch of his life. The lad couldn't straighten his back after that, so he lost his measly job, which had been responsible for him losing his fingers, and now he could hardly walk.

'They all knew he had no father and that his mother was struggling, but instead of helping him, they took advantage of him and beat him down at every opportunity. And, of course, nothing was done about it, just some crass heartless words to all and sundry that the boy had to be made an example of. The poor lad later took his own life, throwing himself into the Thames.

'My father also told me in much the same breath as I'm telling you all now, about a young baron up in the Midlands who took a dislike to one of his stable boys because he wouldn't submit to his sexual advances and he challenged him to a bloody duel of all things. The stable boy declined, telling his master that he'd never put hand to a pistol in his life, but the baron wouldn't let him off the hook and forced him into it. The baron invited all of his cronies along to witness the big one-sided event. Needless to say, the stable boy took a ball of lead to the stomach and died of his wound, and guess what…yeh, you guessed it, no enquiry ever took place into the murder of that boy. He may just as well have shot a rat.' Henry momentarily paused in tensed anger. 'Aye, I'm looking forward to today!'

The outlaws made their way over to the home of George Stokes, monitoring the comings and goings with profound patience from within the murky woodland that concealed them. It was now 7.30 in the evening and darkness had drawn in, so the time was right for them to make their move. James Myers, the youngest of the men, was to knock the door of the well-illuminated mansion. George believed that the chances were good that the same young servant girl who opened the door to his brother would answer it, and upon seeing James, be momentarily more at ease due to his age. The rest of the gang ran with speed down the steep grass-covered hill, their masks hanging loosely around their necks, pistols and sacks tucked tightly into their belts. James sat tight on his horse, waiting until his friends had reached the house and positioned themselves either side of the mansion's elaborate large door before he trotted in a lazy nonchalant fashion down the track alone, in full view of the gentry's home. He dismounted in front of the house and casually walked up the steps to the door, where his friends lay in wait.

Jerry pointed towards the doorbell. 'Ding a ling,' he whispered to James, impatiently hurrying him up.

James rang the bell and, sure enough, a young servant girl answered the door. 'Good evening,' James said. 'My name is John Palmerston. Is your master at home?'

Before a further word was uttered, the men burst through the door while Thomas Ledbury grabbed the girl, placing his hand over her mouth, his knife hovering menacingly under her chin. 'Keep quiet and no harm will come to you, I promise. It's not you we're after,' he whispered to the petrified girl.

The gang moved swiftly through the house with the demeanour of hunting owls stalking their prey. A young male servant stepped out from the parlour carrying the remains of the evening's supper on a large silver platter, as the sound of chatter and laughter reverberated throughout its walls.

Jerry moved in on the unaware servant, stunning him with his old naval cosh, sending him plummeting to the ground, dazed and confused. 'Stay down,' he growled, as he quickly bound the servant's arms and legs before gagging him.

George and Jerry burst into the parlour, masked and armed, confronting its startled occupants. The rest of the outlaws followed, pushing their way in and ordering the servant girl to place herself alongside the Stokes party. Stokes and his wife had been playing cards with family friends and were taken totally by surprise, oblivious to the events that had taken place on the other side of the door.

George Stokes watched, calm and unshaken. The ageing gentry was a hardened calculating man. He observed the intruders from their hats down to their boots, studying the way they moved like a unit without a single word being spoken. *These men have been together many years. It's all second nature to them*, he thought to himself.

James Myers made eye contact with the young man sitting beside George Stokes. It was Stokes's son Charles, whose eyes were flickering with uncontrollable rage. James then looked over at a small gilt clock that sat with pride of place on the room's mantelpiece. Charles Stokes noticeably tensed in his chair as he watched it disappear into James's sack.

James sensed his victim's stress and anxiety, wallowing in the reversal of power and control. He picked up a silver candlestick and turned to look at Charles Stokes before slowly and contemptuously flicking its lit candle on to the floor and then repeating the process with its twin, looking for a reaction to take their eye contact to the next level. However, none came, so the candlesticks were placed into the sack.

The felons then turned their attention to the servants' quarters, as they dragged their bound victim down to the cellar, followed by the Stokes family, their friends and staff, strangely allowing the servant girl to follow at her own free will as if she was an invisible onlooker.

'There'll be a guard on the other side of this door. If you tamper with it, make no mistake, you'll come to harm,' barked Jerry.

George hunted down his brother's delivery of guns and rifles, which had not been moved, lying in the exact same place that Samuel had placed them.

'Their naivety is fucking beyond words,' said George, shaking his head in disbelief as he ogled his discovery. 'Unbelievable, fucking unbelievable!' It brought to mind something his mother once told him as a boy: Just because some people have abundant wealth and are deemed well educated, doesn't mean they're gifted with good old common sense. He smiled to himself. It was yet another occasion where his mother's words had been proved correct.

The collection of guns was removed from the house, bound in bedsheets and tied securely to James Myers's horse. Henry returned from the kitchen clutching a large strongbox containing one hundred and forty guineas. Thomas Ledbury ran over to him, removing a spare sack from his belt, and transferred the coins into it without a word being spoken. Henry returned to the cellar to make sure his incarcerated victims didn't get any ideas.

Tempers had soared and voices were raised. 'You'll all hang for this, you vermin! You don't seem to understand how powerful a man my father is. You'll all be hunted down and made examples of. I promise you this!' shouted Charles Stokes at the top of his voice.

'My, my, I do believe our little friend has taken umbrage with us for relieving them of their belongings.' Henry smirked at Ned. The story of the young boy and the meat pie, with the harsh words 'made examples of' raised his heckles. *They're the same type of people. I wasn't wrong*, he thought to himself. The fuse had been well and truly lit.

'Open the door,' Henry told Ned icily, in no more than a whisper. The door was opened. Charles Stokes was sitting on the floor at the far end of the cellar with the others.

'Stand up,' ordered Henry Watts, to the man who had dared to threaten him. Charles Stokes stayed put. 'I said, stand up.' Henry's words were said in no more than a whisper. Still no movement came from Charles Stokes. Henry and Ned glanced at one another, their mood changing rapidly for the worse.

'Take the bastard's watch,' ordered Henry. Ned moved in but Charles put up resistance. Ned pounced upon him, coshing him with force across the forehead with the butt of his pistol, leaving a deep gaping wound, as he postured over him like a dominant wolf, while Henry seized his gold watch.

They then proceeded to remove the women's jewellery, leaving George Stokes until last, manhandling him and verbally reviling him in front of his family and friends before robbing him of his wedding ring and belongings.

'It's time,' said Henry. No other words were spoken as they headed towards the door.

Yes, they've certainly done this before. They've been together for a long time, thought George Stokes to himself as he watched them take their leave into the misty evening air.

James and Ned took the fully laden horse up to the woodland to disperse the booty amongst all the other horses, while the others made their way back to their horses on foot under the cover of darkness. When they arrived, their steeds were ready and waiting.

George had brought the young servant girl along with him, aware of the fact that she'd seen James Myers's face. 'You'll ride with us for a short while, then you'll walk back to free your master,' George instructed. 'You'll not be able to recognise our friend who knocked your door. It will be vague, very vague. But he'll have brown eyes and brown hair. If we hear otherwise, we'll hunt you down along with your closest ones, do you understand?'

'Yes, sir, I understand,' came the girl's reply.

George dipped into his pocket, removed George Stokes's wife's wedding ring and handed it to the girl. 'You must give this to your master and tell him we dropped it by our horses. You noticed but didn't say a thing and picked it up on your return. It will curry favour for you with your master.'

The girl was taken with them for three miles before being sent on her way back to the manor house.

It was an uncomfortable moment for the outlaws as they rode past the Old Bear Inn. They didn't want to be seen and were relieved when they did so without any misfortune. Jerry led the men off the beaten track to where he and Thomas had been busy earlier in the day. Their little bit of work was about to come into its own.

'Damn,' said Jerry. 'The hole isn't deep enough.' He eyed the sacks and returned his gaze to the shallow grave. 'Go fetch the shovel,' he told Thomas.

Thomas looked at the others despondently. 'Every time we dig it too small, every bloody time!'

George laughed. 'That's not a bad thing. All that tells us is that we've had a good day.'

The men set about enlarging their hideaway and placing the sacks deep into the damp soft ground, before covering it over. The guns were to be taken with them that evening. Their work was finished for the day, so they climbed back on to their horses, cautiously leaving the woodland, before racing into the night.

The following day, Jerry and his gang did what they always did after a robbery – sit back and listen for any information that may find its way back to them. But this time nothing came to light.

Three days passed and their usual sources of information came up with nothing, which was strange. George arrived at the stables behind the Bald Faced Stag.

Jerry was outside grooming his horse. 'Morning, George,' he said, continuing with his grooming as George dismounted.

'Any news?' asked George.

'I was with Henry last night, and we were saying how strange it all is. To be honest, we don't like it,' said Jerry.

George placed himself down on a bench beside Jerry's horse. 'Maybe we should wait this one out a little longer,' he suggested. 'What do you think, Jerry boy?'

'I agree. Something isn't quite right. I can feel it in my gut.'

George nodded, adding, 'Let's leave it a little longer then. Eventually the mole will stick its head out of the dirt.'

'Yeh, let's keep our ears to the ground a little longer.' Agreed Jerry. 'It's all well-hidden down there, so nobody's going to stumble across it. Let's all listen to our instincts.'

George smiled. 'Only a fool wouldn't, my friend, only a fool wouldn't,' he said.

The Bull Inn, Southwark
12 March 1791, 5.30 pm

JERRY AVERSHAW and Henry Watts trotted their horses through the inn's carriage entrance and into its courtyard, dismounted and passed their horses to the ostler. Two young boys watched them from an upstairs window that had been pushed open as wide as it possibly could, their feebly attempted whispers of recognition clearly overheard by the ostler and the two highwaymen.

'Close that window and go about your business!' yelled the ostler. The older of the boys pulled it to but continued to watch.

'Look at 'em, just look at 'em,' said the ostler. 'They couldn't look any more struck with awe if it were the king himself standing here.'

The outlaws laughed as they strolled towards the door. Jerry glanced up at the window and the older boy made eye contact with him and smiled. Jerry returned his smile with a nod and mixed feelings. The boys were without any shadow of a doubt idolising them in the self-same manner that he and Henry had worshipped "Black Jack", John James, in the not-so-distant past.

They could quite easily walk the same path, step by step, if the harsh realities of life determined so. The pillory, jail, the whipping post, even deportation or the gallows. Jerry hoped their opportunities in life were far more favourable than those of his own.

As Jerry and Henry crossed the threshold of the busy bustling inn, they spotted the formidable figure of big George, along with James Myers, standing at the bar chin-wagging with Barclay Cribb the landlord. Their loyal friend had reserved them a table in the corner, its chairs perched upside down on top of it as a message to those who couldn't read. As they approached their table, ale in hand, they became aware of four irksome foundry workers seated close by, their banter tinged with sarcasm and insults to all who strayed within earshot of them. The outlaws ignored them; they had more important things on their minds.

Moments later, Ned Simpson and Thomas Ledbury entered the inn with two impeccably dressed young women. Jerry recognised them instantly – they were courtesans from St George's Fields. He'd met with their acquaintance on several occasions whilst visiting Nancy, his own personal favourite.

They were all in high spirits. The two high tobys had been out with the women all day, squandering no end of their money on them, buying them new dresses and shawls. They were attending the theatre that evening and wanted to look as fine and debonair as they possibly could.

As they passed by the foundry workers, a degrading remark was made by one of the men in the direction of the two women. It didn't go unnoticed, and Ned turned and confronted the man and his friends. The foundry worker eyed Ned from head to toe wistfully, like a spider watching a wasp about to be ensnared into its sticky web.

Those at Jerry's table moved quickly, aligning themselves alongside their cocksure friend. The foundry workers sobered quickly, with the hard realisation that this time they had bitten off far more than they could chew. The men tried to talk their way out of their predicament.

The cowards are like so many, Ned thought to himself. *Brave in numbers, gutless in a one to one.* The bully wasn't going to talk his way out of this one, not with a man whose ideology was a good right-hander is worth a thousand words. A jarring straight right crunched hard into the man's face, breaking his nose and sending a spray of blood across the room. A left hook followed at lightning speed, but it wasn't needed, as the man had crumbled to the ground. The outlaws ordered the man's friends to drag him unceremoniously by the feet out of the bar. Their humiliation was complete.

'Time for you to make tracks, Ned,' said George with a fatherly concern. 'You don't need your evening ruined by a visit from the Runners.' George knew all too well how the silent backstabbers worked, and he wasn't about to hand any kind of revenge to them on a platter. The foundry workers weren't about to be given credit for just going away, licking their wounds and accepting the consequences of just another brawl that didn't quite go to plan.

George's advice wasn't needed; Ned and company were already preparing to take their leave. George's advice that had been drummed into them time and time again over the years was already at work – trust nobody.

As Ned guided the ladies through the crowded inn, Thomas turned and whispered into George's ear. 'Any chance of a loan until the morning George.

41

I've overspent and don't want to look bad.' George raised his eyebrows and gave him a glum look of dismay, before delving deep into his pocket and giving him all he had.

'Thanks, mate. It will be back in your pocket first thing tomorrow.'

'Make sure it is,' George replied with the tone of a disenchanted father rather than a friend.

'I must be heading off myself lads,' George added. 'Seeing I'm now potless.'

'Aw, don't worry yourself about that. Stay and join us for supper. We're going to eat soon. Come on,' said Henry. 'Jenny won't mind. She's not one of life's sulkers.' Henry handed George another ale. 'Let the evening begin!'

Jenny Berwick knew all too well that the man she wished to share the rest of her life with was no angel dropped down from the heavens to enrich her life. She also knew there would be just as many bad times ahead as there would be good, aware that George was a very active criminal, running the blade's edge from one day to the next. She also understood that his fun-loving friends were no different, and she had adapted the knack of placing it to the back of her mind, so as not to torment herself to the border of insanity. Instead, she focused on the nicer side, the big jovial man enjoying a drink in the evening and chewing the cud with his friends and their non-stop humour. How he earned his living was never discussed and asking was never going to attract an honest answer. No, best not ask. Let sleeping dogs lie.

George was fully aware of and understood her uneasiness, which was why he'd promised her the money for their little tavern that was going to materialise in the not-so-distant future.

The Bull Inn, Southwark
The Following Morning

UNFORTUNATELY FOR the three outlaws, who had spent the night at the Bull, their overindulgence the previous evening had led to considerable overspending on people they didn't really know, which had placed them in the self-same embarrassing predicament as that of Thomas. 'How are we going to pay Barclay?' groaned Henry, sitting on the edge of his bed with his head resting heavily in his hands.

A croaky voice, sounding just as sorry for itself, reluctantly perked up. It was Jerry. 'Give me a minute and I'll go and have a word with him.' He gingerly pulled on his boots and made his way down to face the music.

Barclay was cleaning the bar, while his wife was with one of the barmaids, mopping the ale-soaked floor, which had been violently assaulted by Jerry and his malevolent entourage seven hours earlier.

'Morning, Barclay,' said Jerry with a hint of uncomfortable embarrassment. 'Hear me out before you hit the roof.' The landlord looked at him with an 'I know what's coming next' look.

'We don't have enough pelf in our pockets to pay you your dues,' Jerry continued. 'But if you give us the rest of the morning, we'll return and pay you.'

'Today?' asked Barclay hopefully.

'Yes, today. On my word.'

'That's fine, Jerry, no problem,' came the landlord's reply, realising that his options of retrieving his money were limited to say the least.

Soon afterwards, the three highwaymen made their way out of the back door to the stables. Barclay, his wife and the barmaid watched the motley crew from a window, shaking their heads and tutting, interspersed with spasmodic outbursts of laughter, as the fragile-looking threesome clumsily tried to pull their aching hungover carcasses on to their horses.

'Three beyond beautiful horses and three worn-out wretches.' Quipped Barclay's wife.

'I know,' chuckled Barclay. 'Nobody can say my ale is watered down.'

The three men trotted off in the direction of Borough High Street, making their way to Kennington Common. Upon reaching their destination they continued to trot their horses casually along the busy Kennington Road, following the line of the rustic fencing that penned in the sheep and cattle. They looked like race horses walking the course at Ascot before a race.

As they approached the site of the gallows, Jerry observed a lone figure approaching from afar, so he reached into his inside pocket and removed his spyglass. It was a sentimental item that he carried with him at all times, stolen from a toff on his first outing as a highwayman. It was once a good conversation piece with his close-knit group of friends, who he would tell, much to his own amusement, about how his well-heeled victim was so absorbed in viewing the scenery from his chaise with his spyglass pressed firmly to his eye that he didn't see him coming until it was too late.

Jerry loved the way the spyglass opened and retracted to such a small size, whereupon you could place it comfortably into your pocket. He loved its tactility and admired its craftsmanship. It had been made by Cary of London and its guilt metal and cloth finish made it a keeper for him. Henry referred to it as Jerry's little toy of mischief. As Jerry viewed the stranger advancing towards them, he decided he was worth a look, instantly pulling his crepe mask up over his face and descending upon him at lightning speed. Henry glanced towards George, po-faced and momentarily stunned at Jerry's sudden change of pace from that of a hungover sloth to a hungry hunting wolf. Henry and George simultaneously pulled their masks up over their unshaven faces and followed in hot pursuit, as Jerry closed in on the man, head down.

Jerry drew his pistol. 'Hand over what's yours! What you have on your person is now mine!'

The highwayman's two friends approached, levelling their horses either side of the petrified soul, who was dumbfounded by the brazen audacity of doing such a dirty deed in broad daylight under the shadow of the gallows. The foreboding structure had no apparent deterrent effect upon them, and the man resigned himself to the fact that the situation was out of his hands. Without as much as a grumble, he handed over his precious belongings to the hardened criminals.

'Thank you, and good day to you,' Jerry said. 'Now turn and head back in the same direction as you came. Don't look back and don't make any attempt to follow us or it will end in bad repercussions for you and your close ones.'

The man turned and trotted away, his body tense as if in anticipation of a gunshot being discharged into his back. His state of mind was enough for him to break into a gallop to widen the distance, without any thoughts of peering over his shoulder.

Barclay Cribb couldn't hide the look of relief that was etched so predominantly across his purple-cheeked face as Jerry, George and Henry returned to his inn.

'Back so soon?' He chirped up with a smile. The three men pulled out some chairs and sat down at a table as if they had just finished a shift down the docks.

'Three lovely coffees wouldn't go amiss, Barclay,' said Jerry. The landlord smiled with the expectation of good things coming his way.

Jerry looked around before leaning over the bar. 'This should cover things,' he murmured as he passed Barclay a gold pocket watch. 'It might be advisable to keep that bright shiny little thing in a dark place for a while. It's still glowing hot.'

'I will, Jerry, I will,' said Barclay with a greedy smile. 'If you can stomach it, do you all fancy some breakfast?'

The Talbot Inn, Southwark
14 March 1791, 6 pm

THOMAS LEDBURY and Ned Simpson sat eating their mutton pies and enjoying their ale, whilst cocking an inquisitive ear in the direction of three young apprentices from the *London Daily Post* who were discussing "the robbery by the gallows" story as their publication called it.

'It must be Avershaw and his gang. Who else could it be?' said one of the young men, his friends nodding passionately in agreement.

Ned Simpson turned in his chair by the bar, still eating his pie. 'No, no, gents. How can it possibly be him? I've just been having that same discussion with my good friend here. When Avershaw descends upon his poor victims, he cusses them with the words "damn your eyes"… pardon my language. If you ask any coachman or post boy who's fallen foul of this awful individual, they'll tell you the very same thing. They know when they've come face to face with him and his associates. No, they must be another bunch of itinerants.'

'A very interesting point you make, sir. An avenue of consideration we've overlooked,' the same man replied.

'Yes, worth a thought,' said Ned as he turned back to his friend with a lacklustre expression scrolled across his face.

Thomas looked at him, woefully shaking his head. 'Itinerants? Where did you get that fancy word from?'

'Don't be so cheeky. I've rubbed shoulders with the well-educated from time to time. One of them actually called me that very word as I robbed him.'

'Blimey,' said Thomas, 'the things you learn. Life's one big school, innit.'

The Bald-Faced Stag Inn, Putney Vale
17 March 1791, 9.30 am

BIG GEORGE Alston slumped into his favourite chair beside the roaring log fire, burying his head with deep concentration into the *London Daily Post*. His concentration was momentarily broken by the sound of footsteps clumping slowly down the stairs. It was Jerry.

'Bacon, eggs and a coffee, please, Jack,' Jerry asked in no more than a whisper before joining his friend.

'Look at this,' said George, showing his newspaper to Jerry before reading it aloud: 'Forty guineas reward will be given for each and every thief who robbed the household of George Stokes, proprietor of Stockton Manor, Cobham, Surrey on the evening of 10 March 1791. He's even given rough descriptions of us and James's horse.'

'It looks like the servant girl has taken heed of my words. She hasn't given an accurate description of James,' said Jerry.

'Hmm, maybe…or just maybe she's taken a perverse shine to him,' said George with a grin. His broad shoulders bounced up and down uncontrollably as he chuckled, dismissing Jerry's thoughts of intimidation being the key factor over that of good old-fashioned compatibility.

George drew a deep breath, his chuckles sobering to a more serious tone. 'It's time to dig it all up, Jerry. Me and the lads have bills to pay. The creditors are knocking on Thomas's door, young Jim owes people and my Jenny's giving me grief about the tavern. I don't blame her none, as I'm not getting any younger and, like you, I can't work for anyone. I never could take orders and I sure as hell ain't starting now. I've got to accumulate enough money for our tavern, and at this moment in time it's sitting in some woodland in the back of beyond.'

'Listen, George, I don't feel good about this one. There's a bad moon rising, I can feel it in my bones. I think we should keep away from that neck of the woods for some considerable time, and after reading this it only makes my thoughts more justified. Their first port of call will be the Old Bear Inn, and we know descriptions of a sort have been given. To be honest I'm surprised they're so vague.'

'Aye, some people shy away and don't want to get involved, especially if they don't need the reward money or they're not of that mentality,' said George. 'It was busy in there that day, so maybe Stokes doesn't cut the popular figure around there as one would think. Maybe he's a selfish man who doesn't give any thought to the locals. After all, there seems to be quite a lot of that type around, so it's a possibility that should be given some consideration.'

'Hmm, possibly, George, possibly, but I still think we should let things settle. Maybe time and other factors in life will dampen his enthusiasm to pursue it any further but, for the time being, it makes sense to sit tight.'

'Do you trust me, Jerry?' asked George, looking at his friend with an inquisitive eye.

'Of course, with my life, why?'

George pondered for a while over his next line of thought, before continuing. 'How about I give you a proposition. If you and Henry agree to us going back to get it and to return it to a safe house, that being the home of my Samuel in Wimbledon, we can cut our shares from there under the security of his roof.'

'You've been giving this some deep thought, haven't you, George?'

'Aye, I have, and if we get caught, Henry and yourself are as safe as houses. You know you can trust us not to utter a word.'

The adjoining stable door creaked open, interrupting their discussion. It was Henry, so George explained his proposition to him.

'There's a problem here, George,' Henry said. 'If things were to go wrong, we would not only lose our friends to the hangman, but the spoils would all be returned to Stokes. What do you say to leaving the silver in the ground and taking everything else? It would make me feel a little more comfortable about it and, if all goes well, we can return some time further down the line to retrieve it. That way we can still have something to line our pockets if things go wrong and, of course, Stokes wouldn't be completely avenged. I know his type when it comes to money; it will rankle with him till his dying day whether he admits it or not. Also, George, I don't think it's a good thing to take James along with you. The servant girl saw his face, so leave him at home; better safe than sorry.'

'Fine,' agreed George. 'Just Ned, Thomas and me it is. We'll make our way over there this evening.'

The Green Man Inn, Putney Heath
That Evening, 7.30 pm

HEAVY RAIN bounced off the windows of the inn, aided by a harsh cutting northerly wind, as George stared out at the conditions he would soon be amongst. There wasn't as much as a glint of despondency or frustration in his eyes. His mindset was as strong as an ox, and nothing Mother Nature could throw at him was going to deter him from making that long unforgiving journey in such treacherous elements to retrieve what wasn't rightfully his.

He headed, along with Ned and Thomas, to the stables, where they mounted their horses that had been made ready by the ostler, and took to the dark, wet, windy highway. They made their way as best they could, arriving at their destination later than expected. As they approached the dense woodland close by the large imposing oak tree, Ned noticed two horsemen in the distance heading towards them.

'Keep moving,' Ned warned the others. 'Don't turn off. Look up ahead.'

'What's the fucking chances,' mumbled George angrily as he pulled his rain-drenched hat down over his eyes.

'We're no more than a breath away from the Old Bear Inn. They've probably come from there,' said Ned.

As they passed the two strangers they nodded in acknowledgement, using the conditions of the driving rain as a prime excuse to avoid eye contact. They continued onwards until the men were out of sight before turning in their tracks and cautiously, like hunted deer, sweeping nervously into the woodland, aware that the naked trees were unable to totally conceal them from prying eyes.

As they dismounted, Thomas whispered, 'Listen.' They stood motionless beside their horses. The two men they had passed moments earlier had returned.

They could hear them talking to one another, laughing, but their words were incomprehensible.

The outlaws remained standing as still as the trees themselves and waited until the clip clop of the horses' hooves drifted silently into the distance, before making their way over to their grave of ill-gotten plunder.

Spades clenched tightly in hand, they dug hard and fast, retrieving the damp, mud-sodden sacks that weren't deserving of the contents that laid within, before attaching them to their horses.

'It's going to be a long journey, George. We can't use the road now that we know people are about,' groaned Thomas despondently.

'Aye, slow and easy. Away from over-inquisitive nosy types,' said George.

They rode slowly and cautiously, as far away from the road as they possibly could without losing sight of it, following the most direct route back to Wimbledon. They picked up speed when they were out in the open and at their most vulnerable, relying on their vigilance and good fortune to see anyone approaching before they saw them.

As they approached the outskirts of Wimbledon Common, George tried to lift the spirits of his two young friends. 'Not far now, boys. Just one more mile or so and we'll be at Samuel's.'

'Good. I hope he has a good fire burning and some food and ale ready upon our arrival,' said Thomas optimistically. 'Aye, for sure lads, for sure,' replied George. The three men began to feel a little more relaxed, despite being cold, tired and exhausted.

Suddenly, without warning, a gunshot rang out, shattering the tranquillity of the night. A large group of men on horseback charged towards them, the heavy thud of horses' hooves pounding the ground in unison as they rushed towards their startled foe. George drew his pistol and fired, but it flashed in the pan. A shot was returned. It found its mark, wounding George in his right shoulder, burying itself deep into his flesh, rendering his arm useless, as he fell from his horse.

'Don't move. You're under arrest!' It was George Stokes, accompanied by seven armed men and an officer of the law. One of the men was instantly recognised by all three outlaws. It was the notorious thief-taker Mathew Caplin. They were caught red-handed, no excuses, no way out.

George looked at Stokes whilst clenching his gaping wound. 'How did you find us?' he asked.

Stokes remained mounted on his horse, looking down on his felled, stricken, prisoner. 'You passed my friend, the landlord of the Old Bear Inn. He couldn't see you clearly, but he recognised your horses. He's very good at placing a horse with its owner, it's a bit of a gift. He'd seen you in his establishment before you decided to rob my home.'

Another of the men, still mounted, spoke up, smirking with satisfaction, 'I told you that you would pay for what you did. Nobody robs my father and lives to tell the tale.' It was the son of George Stokes, Charles.

Kennington Common, London
26 March 1791

GEORGE ALSTON, Ned Simpson and Thomas Ledbury were true to their word, and refused to tell who was in their company on the night of the robbery when they were questioned at the Croydon Assizes. They were tried and sentenced to death, with the added humiliation of being hung in chains and displayed in public as a deterrent to others after their executions. They were to be hung on Kennington Common and thereafter gibbeted on Wimbledon Common, on the very spot of their apprehension.

Within nine days of their capture, George, Ned and Thomas found themselves climbing on to the death cart in Newgate Prison, to be paraded through London's busy streets, dressed no differently to that of the gentry they had robbed. There wasn't a glimmer of apprehension or fear between the three of them; it was beyond unnatural.

George drifted into his own little world, the noise of the marauding crowd seemingly having no impact on his deep final thoughts. He would never see his Jenny again; their dream was over. He wondered whether she would continue the rest of her days as a barmaid. Would she find herself another man? And if she did, what would he look like? He wanted to weep, but he couldn't. It would have been misinterpreted as fear and cowardice in his final moments of life.

He snapped out of his spell and looked at his two friends. *So young and yet so fucking hard*, he thought. They were resigned to their fate as if it was part of the natural circle of life. He'd been around these young men for so long that he took for granted how mentally and physically tough they were. He watched them as they performed to the crowd, resigned to their fate. They were to show no signs of remorse, nor give anyone the slightest taste of satisfaction. They were certainly going to look death straight back in the eye and say, 'Damn your eyes, fucker!'

George cracked a smile as he shouted. 'Top of the tree, boys. Top of the tree!' The crowd continued to cheer. They loved brave men who put on a good show and died gamely. They were on the outlaws' side, for what it was worth.

As the prayers were being read, Ned and Thomas set about cussing Stokes and his family. George stayed staunch and silent. His wound still wept constantly, staining the exterior of his coat. He made eye contact with a man no more than twenty feet away in the crowd, it was Jerry. Henry was beside him.

The ropes were placed around the three men's necks as Jerry and George locked eyes on each other. Jerry mouthed, 'You'll be avenged, my friend. Stokes will pay,' to George, who continued his intense eye contact with his friend as he, Ned and Thomas leapt from the cart at the same time before the hangman's whip had a chance to touch the horse's tail. Their necks snapped instantly.

The men's pre-planned jump was yet another well-thought-over agreement to deny Stokes his moment of twisted glory. His fifteen minutes of perverted pleasure as they slowly choked whilst dangling before his eyes had been denied him.

A part of Jerry died that day. He didn't stay to see his friends being cut down, although he'd paid some large men to run forward and hang on to his friends' legs if things didn't go to plan. Fortunately, they weren't needed.

******

The thought of his friends being hung in chains on Wimbledon Common rankled heavily with Jerry. The following morning, as he lay in his bed, part of him didn't want to get up and face the world where he wasn't going to see George, Ned or Thomas ever again. His everyday routine had suddenly changed beyond all recognition and he felt anxious and even a little scared, like a man trapped beneath the water, unable to reach the surface in a bad dream. He felt that same kind of helplessness but this time it was for real. His friends had been reduced to memories that would gradually fade but still give him hurt and sadness till the day of his own passing.

Jerry turned his thoughts to Stokes, trying to get his head around the man's logic and way of thinking. Why didn't they show some leniency? Just a little clemency. If a life had been taken, then he could understand why they would want to even the score, but that hadn't been the case. He's a very well-connected man so he could have, without any shadow of a doubt, had them transported to Australia, but he didn't even try. Jerry's sorrow was battling with his rage, and the rage was beginning to take control of his emotions. There was a heavy-handed knock on the door. 'Go away,' came Jerry's uncourteous reply to the unwanted visitor.

'Let me in Jerry. It's me, Henry. I'm with James.' Jerry walked over to the door and turned the key in the lock, before returning to his bed.

Henry opened the door and walked in, followed closely by James. Jerry was lying back on his bed, his hands resting behind his head as he studied James, whose eyes were puffy and red. Jerry could feel his pain.

Henry seemed to be holding it together far better than his two friends. 'I'm not sure if it has sunk in on me at the moment, it still seems so unreal,' he said.

James looked at Henry, saying, 'He was like a father to me, Henry. I never really knew my father. You know that George was always there for me, through thick and thin, but now he's been taken from me. And Ned and Thomas were like my older brothers, fighting my battles for me until I was old enough to take care of myself, and, even then, they were always close at hand.'

Henry placed his arm around his grief-stricken friend. 'You have us in your corner always and forever, James, don't forget that. You'll never go without. We're family.'

Jerry nodded at Henry's words with approval and said, 'Get Jack to bring some food and ale up here, James. After all, we're not going anywhere this evening. Oh, and get him to ask old Ralph to put the horses away for the night while you're there.'

The Following Morning
27 March 1791

JERRY SAT within the confines of his room, with only the repetitive tick tock of the mantle clock to intrude on his thoughts. The peaceful atmosphere was about to end, though, as Henry's slumber on the floor next to him was broken by the sound of Jerry pulling on his boots.

'Where are you going?' Henry asked with concern, as he snapped into life quickly.

'I'm going to cut them down,' Jerry replied. Henry looked at his friend, whose eyes looked vacant and whose hands were trembling uncontrollably. Jerry's state of mind was irrational and worrying.

'Just wait a minute, Jerry. Listen to what I have to say. We're going to do this, but it needs to be given more thought. If we rush in now, we'll be seen and caught quicker than you can pull on your boots and end up hanging beside them. If we take our time and get it right, they'll be resting in their graves away from the ghouls soon enough. Trust me.' Henry's words made sense.

'What do you have in mind?' asked Jerry, questioning whether his friend had even a fragment of a plan or these were just hollow pacifying words.

'I'm going to visit Lance Andrews at his farriers. His cousin builds the gibbets, so he can tell us about the quickest and easiest way to get them down, and also supply the tools to do it'

Jerry nodded solemnly. 'Let's go see Lance,' he whispered. The two men woke James Myers and made their way over to their friend's place of work, which sat within a stone's throw of St Paul's Cathedral.

Lance Andrews broke away from his work upon seeing his friends tethering their horses beside his stable. 'Hello, Henry,' he said, as he marched towards them briskly, before nodding towards Jerry and James with a knowing mournful smile. Jerry nodded back, his stern face etched with stress. James was no different.

'We need your help and advice, Lance,' said Henry, cutting to the chase.
'How can I help you, Henry?'

'We're looking to cut down our friends tonight, and we need your advice on the best way to go about it,' said Henry anxiously, his eyes focused on his friend, hoping for a positive reply. Lance broke away from Henry's penetrating eyes, looking to the ground to ease his discomfort. It was clear he wasn't going to give the answer they hoped for.

'I've been told this fellow Stokes still has an axe to grind,' Lance said. 'He knows they weren't the only ones who entered his home and robbed him. My cousin told me the gibbeting of George, Ned and Thomas is a lure to try to draw in the others, so he's expecting you to make an attempt to cut down your friends.' Henry turned to Jerry with a "told you so" look. Jerry ignored him.

'I'm glad you're all here,' Lance continued. 'It's been playing on my mind. I've been trying to get in touch, but nobody knew of your whereabouts. Apparently, Stokes has continued to hire Mathew Caplin the thief-taker and his men to discreetly watch over the gibbets from afar, in order to take by surprise anyone who tries to cut them down. You must all keep away from that area, day and night. These people are serious.'

Lance looked at his frustrated friends, mulling over in his mind whether he should inform them of the further bad news he had to bestow upon them. He decided to jump in with both feet and tell them. 'I've thought long and hard about what I'm about to tell you, and in the long term I think it's the right thing to do. The last thing in the world I'd wish upon my friends is more hurt. But it has to be said that if you do decide to go over there, you must be prepared for what you see. They've not only hung them in chains, they've also tarred their bodies to preserve them, solely for the benefit of their fellow robbers. It was George Stokes's idea yet again. He thought it would lead to emotional anger, which of course would lead to you thoughtlessly rushing in and falling into his trap.'

Henry rested his hand on Lance's shoulder, telling him, 'You're a true friend, Lance. I'll visit you soon in the hope of you having any further information that may help us.' The big farrier nodded to his friends affectionately as they turned their horses and trotted away to ponder their next move.

The Green Man Inn, Putney Heath
27 March 1791, 6.30 pm

'EVENING, ARTHUR. Is Jenny around?' asked Jerry, whilst removing his hat and brushing off the excess rain from his coat.

'No, she's gone back to Carlisle to mourn amongst her family. She won't be coming back. She's done with this place. There's nothing to keep her here anymore.'

'How was she?' asked Jerry, with a hint of discomfort and embarrassment in his voice for asking the obvious.

'She couldn't speak. I haven't seen anything quite like it before. I've seen tragedy, devastation and sorrow – good heavens, I've been there myself when my Anne passed away. That terrible feeling of loneliness that takes over you, even when you're surrounded by family and friends. I think poor Jenny was in that very moment. She just packed her belongings and left. She didn't even ask for her wages. I had to scrape it together on the quick and put it in her bag. It's terribly sad, as those two really had something special between them. The way she spoke I think they had plans to get married in the not-so-distant future. She even hinted at starting a family before George got too old.' Arthur smiled. 'I don't know how George would have felt about that. Life can be so bloody cruel.'

Jerry took his ale and walked over to the window, taking a good hard look across the heath. He thought of the little chat Henry had with Lance that morning and realised that Henry was right, they would have been at the mercy of Stokes if they had listened to him. He would have led them straight into a trap, like lobsters in a pot. But at least they now knew that Stokes didn't know who else was at his home that evening and even if he did have his suspicions he sure as hell had no proof. He was relying entirely on finding out who was there that day by who tried to cut down George, Ned and Thomas.

Yeh, Henry was right, Jerry thought. *Sit back and wait. Stokes isn't going to pay these men forever. As soon as they realise we're not going to turn up they'll call it a day and then we can move in and give our friends their burial.*

The Bald-Faced Stag Inn, Putney Vale
4 April 1791, 7.30 pm

THE WEATHER-BEATEN figure of a darkly dressed man followed by another man, slightly smaller in stature, passed through the smoke-filled, candlelit room. Men and women alike were talking louder than usual, fuelled by the excessive consumption of ales and spirits. This was no place for a gentleman of good standing and, moreover, even less so for a respectable lady of good reputation.

The two men looked dishevelled and tired. They had obviously been on the road many hours. The smaller of the two called over to the innkeeper, a stout middle-aged man with thick silver hair combed back in a no-fuss style and a complexion that told you he was partial to sampling his own range of fine ales.

'Get old Ralph to take care of our horses. And get a doctor. My friend isn't feeling well.' The two men climbed the dark stairwell to their lodgings.

'Go look for a doctor,' the landlord despondently told a young boy of no more than twelve years. The boy leapt from his chair, immediately pulled on his threadbare coat and rushed out of the door of the inn into the cold evening air. He crossed the muddy road, whilst huddling deeper into his coat in a vain attempt to shield himself from the harsh wind that drove mercilessly towards him as he made the half-mile trek to the nearest village. After a short passage of time the boy returned. He'd done well and had someone with him.

'I'm Doctor William Roots,' came the stranger's bold announcement to the landlord, in a clear well-educated voice, not often encountered in his establishment.

'Upstairs,' said the landlord, as he gestured at the boy to lead the doctor up the stairs and along its dark, dusty corridor.

'This is the room, sir,' said the boy, pointing towards the door in a respectful way that suggested someone of grand importance was residing on the other side, before knocking heavily on the door and taking his leave.

'Who is it?' called a disgruntled voice from inside the room.

'I'm Doctor William Roots. You called for my assistance.' The door was opened.

'Please come in, sir,' said a young man of no more than twenty years of age. 'My friend has taken a turn for the worse. He almost collapsed on the stairs earlier.'

Doctor Roots looked across the room towards a fully clothed man stretched out on a bed in the corner. He approached him, placing his bag on a small table close by, before examining him.

'You have a fever, sir. You need to be bled.' Doctor Roots explained the procedure to his patient as he opened his bag and removed his scarificator. 'Please bring me some clean towels and a bowl,' the doctor instructed the young man, who immediately complied. The doctor proceeded to bleed his patient.

'Sleep as upright as you can. You need plenty of rest. And keep this room as warm as possible at all times,' the doctor instructed, while bandaging the open wounds. 'If you need me again, I can be reached at this address.' The doctor handed his patient one of his calling cards, before briskly writing out his bill and giving it to his patient's friend, who instantly paid him his dues.

'You're from Fulham, sir?' enquired the patient as he pulled himself up in his bed, taking the doctor's advice.

'Yes, not too far away,' came the reply.

'Far enough, sir, far enough,' the patient said. 'Let my friend here escort you back under his protection. You don't know who you may encounter on your journey back on such an overcast evening.'

'That's very kind of you, but it won't be necessary,' replied the doctor. 'You don't have to worry about me, for I fear no man, even if I were to meet with Avershaw himself.' The patient smiled at the doctor and bade him farewell as he went on his way.

The patient's friend watched from the window as the lonely figure, clutching his bag, made his way from the inn. 'I hope the boys aren't operating tonight,' he said matter-of-factly, as he watched the doctor make his way along the road.

'Well at least he won't meet with Avershaw himself this evening, will he,' said the patient woefully, as he leaned back in his bed.

'No. No,' said his friend, still watching from the window with a smile. 'No, Jerry, he won't be meeting with you tonight. That's for sure.'

******

Jerry's recovery was slow, but to all around him it was nothing less than a godsend. They watched him from day to day, struggling beyond all comprehension with the waiting game. And his misfortune of contracting a fever was the deciding factor in making him do just that…sit back and wait.

He seemed a little more at ease. His thinking was less erratic and compulsive, and more logical. He wondered to himself: *Would the landlord of the Old Bear Inn be able to recognise James's horse?* He and Henry were safe enough because they both owned black mares, but James's horse, on the other hand, had facial and body markings that the sharp-eyed landlord may well have observed. It wasn't a risk they could afford to take. The horse must be replaced. The sound of someone talking to old Ralph, the ostler, stole him from his thoughts. He peered through the window to see a slim swarthy man handing his horse over to the ageing ostler and swaggering with an exaggerated roll of the shoulders towards the inn. Jerry placed himself down in his armchair awaiting the arrival of the news.

'Hello, Jerry,' said the man as he walked through the door, which had been left open awaiting his arrival.

Jerry pulled himself out of his chair to greet the man. 'Hello, Joe.'

Joe looked at his friend with an understanding smile, aware of the nightmare he'd just been through, a journey that the strongest of souls would find it impossible to come away from unscathed. *Like a treasured toy soldier that's been broken and repaired. Still functional but never to be the same thereafter*, he thought to himself.

But Joe chose his words carefully. 'Stay strong. We can't afford to lose you too brother. The loss of George, Ned and Thomas has taken a heavy toll on all of us. If anything happened to you, it would mean the beginning of the end for all of us.'

They sat down and talked, and then talked some more, reminiscing about past mischievous deeds they had partaken of with their late friends. Joe Lorrison carried the nickname "Jumping Joe" from childhood when he would rob carts and wagons as they made their way through the busy London streets. He would quickly jump into the backs of the carts and throw out anything of value to his confederates who were close at hand. Jerry, Henry, Ned and Thomas were more often than not Joe's closest allies, and after they determined what to keep and what to pass on, their next stop was a visit to George, who fenced the rest.

Jumping Joe resided in Southwark, where he was known as a most daring depredator to the city of London's public. He was once tried for the murder of a watchman, though he was acquitted because of insufficient evidence, but it was generally believed throughout the neighbourhood that he was guilty of the crime.

Jerry explained the dilemma of James's horse to Joe.

'I can take it to the horse and cattle market over in Chelmsford this Monday if you like,' said Joe. 'There's always good business going on over there. I'll make a point of selling it to someone from further afield and get a fair price.'

Jerry smiled. A great weight had been lifted from his shoulders. One less problem to occupy his mind.

Jumping Joe sold James's horse and returned on the Tuesday morning to give Jerry the money from the sale. It was clearly apparent with these men that there was such a thing as loyalty amongst thieves.

******

Three days more passed but it seemed more like six to Henry Watts. His anxiety and recurring lack of tolerance was becoming as acute as that of Jerry, so he decided to pay a visit to Lance Andrews.

'Hello, Lance, any news?' Henry asked the farrier. 'Caplin's men are still at the gallows, Henry. I took a ride out there myself yesterday evening.' Lance hesitated as if giving himself enough time to choose the correct words. His blue eyes glazed over and softened until tears developed in each corner. He shook his head profusely, trying to pull himself together before bowing his head and pinching away the tears with his thumb and forefinger, then continued.

'I wish I'd never looked!' He snapped, scolding himself for his over-inquisitive actions. The hideous sight of his lifelong friends' bodies hanging degradingly in chains was undoubtedly going to repeat itself in the form of many a restless night for a long time to come.

Andrews went on: 'They think they're being clever with their scouts riding back and forth, pretending to be ordinary folk going about their daily chores. I didn't see any of Caplin's men about, but they can't be far away because these scouts were carrying hunting horns so they could sound the alarm if anyone made a move to cut the bodies down.'

'Thanks, Lance. Your eyes are still as sharp as ever. Many a person wouldn't have picked up on the hunting horns,' said Henry, as his gaze drifted across the yard to a horse tethered in the corner. 'Is that horse yours?' he asked, nodding towards a fine chestnut stallion.

'Yes, I acquired him for myself only yesterday.'

'My, my, Lance, you certainly do still have a sharp eye. He's a real out and outer.'

'He belonged to Sir Henry Jacobs, who passed away suddenly a short time ago. Shame. He was a good man, a proper gent. He was only forty-two years of age.' Lance winced at his thoughtless words, with the realisation that their friends had been even younger.

'His family invited me over to their home to ask if I knew of a respectable buyer for him.' Lance added. 'They were aware that I'd always admired him. I think it was their way of giving me the first opportunity of purchasing him. Their assumption was right because I bought him there and then, with the agreement that he was for me, but now, when push comes to shove, I look at my old friend Jimmy and think to myself, you still have many a good year in you, and the situation made me realise he's not just any old horse, he's my companion, and we can't be separated.'

Henry walked around the handsome stallion, patting him gently as he did so. 'James needs a good horse. Will you sell it to him?' he asked.

'Maybe. If I ask the Jacobs family and explain my dilemma with my own horse, they might possibly agree to me selling him on to James for the same price that I paid. That way I won't upset them, and I'll keep a good working relationship with them. I suppose I'll have to tell them a white lie about what James does for a living and of course it obviously can't go to work with James, you must understand.'

'It goes without saying, Lance. It goes without saying.' Henry agreed.

'Then I'll do my best.' Lance promised.

Henry gave a strained smile before bidding Lance farewell. 'I'll see you in a couple of days, my friend. Keep your ear to the ground and go about your business. Don't take any more risks for us.'

Lance nodded. 'Will do, Henry. Will do.'

The Bald-Faced Stag Inn, Putney Vale
26 April 1791, 10.30 am

JERRY'S RECOVERY was coming to a close. He didn't feel as tired – as a matter of fact, he felt better than he had done for quite some time. He put it down to plenty of rest and keeping away from London's smoke and fog-enriched air that hung over it constantly, like a tormenting thunder cloud. The little fire inside of him was now burning brightly and George Stokes was sitting predominantly at the top of his priority list.

'Where do you think Henry has got to? He said he'd be here for ten o'clock,' asked an increasingly peeved James Myers, as he sat by the fire with Jerry, playing cards.

'Don't worry yourself. He'll be here soon enough,' said Jerry with a knowing expression etched across his face. 'He happened to mention to me that you were going over to Lance's with him at midday.'

'Aye, he told me of a capital chestnut stallion that you couldn't better that's in Lance's possession and he wants me to go over and run my eyes over it and hopefully purchase it from him if it takes my fancy,' said James.

'Well, let's hope the previous owner's family are happy with Lance's reasons and answers,' said Jerry in an attempt to keep his overanxious friend's feet firmly on the ground. 'You can take my horse when Henry arrives. She could do with a run.'

'Thanks, Jerry. I was going to suggest that to you myself, as she does need the exercise.'

Jerry smiled. 'Well thank you for being so thoughtful,' he said sarcastically.

James abruptly jumped from his chair as if it were infested with a thousand fleas.

'Where are you going?' asked Jerry.

'I'm going to ask Ralph to saddle up your horse for eleven o'clock. I don't want to keep Henry waiting when he arrives.'

James's excitement was all too clear to see. Jerry was happy that his friend's mind was momentarily distracted from their perpetual nightmare. He was like an excited schoolboy. Jerry just hoped James wasn't going to be let down with the news that the horse couldn't be sold to him.

Lance Andrews's Farriers
Watling Street, London
The Same Day, 12 Noon

'THE JACOBS family have agreed to the sale of the horse if you're interested,' Lance informed James.

'It was a gruelling haul persuading them, I can tell you, but after careful consideration they took into account that you're a close friend of mine, and after letting it be known that he'll be shod by myself, and myself only, they succumbed to my subtle pressure.'

Lance raised a self-satisfied smile, before adding, 'They took much comfort in knowing he would be under my watchful eye on a regular basis. They told me his well-being must be of paramount importance to me and, if anything otherwise occurs, I should let them know immediately. That's how strongly they feel about him going to someone who loves him as much as their father did, and if anything happens to you James, God forbid, whereupon he's left without that security and protection, then he must be returned to me for the same price he was purchased. I need that in writing with your signature sitting proudly beneath it. Not that I distrust you in any way, but if you're not around I'll have the proof he's to be returned to me. Things can't be taken for granted.'

James nodded in carefree agreement. 'Come on, let me see this treasure you're all making such a fuss about. I want to see how capable he is.'

Lance gave a proud, confident grin as he made his way into the stables. 'Give me a moment,' he said. 'He has to be saddled and bridled.'

James shuffled his feet with confounded impatience. A nervous twitch of the nose, with a mild purse of the lips became apparent, much to Henry's amusement. It was something he'd never witnessed before in all their time together as friends. This horse meant more to James than anyone could ever have imagined. It was a moment of solace in a world that seemed to be kicking at him from all angles.

Lance led the stallion through the stable's immaculately kept doors, grinning from ear to ear like a proud father showing off his new born child for the very first time. James couldn't believe the vision that stood before him. It was beyond his wildest dreams.

'His name is Archie and he's four years old,' Lance explained.

James stood awestruck. 'Archie you say.'

'Yes, apparently it's a play on the word archer,' said Lance. 'The story told to me was that when Sir Henry first laid eyes on him, his wife looked and said, "Look at his power. He's as strong as an archer's arm." A fitting name, don't you think?'

'Yes indeed. I can't argue with that,' said James, stroking the horse reassuringly as he looked into his eyes. 'You're sad and confused and feel unwanted. Your world has been turned upside down and you don't understand why. Just like my old friend Ned Simpson.' The sad situation that had brought them together made James want to bond with Archie even stronger than before.

'Can he remain stabled here, Lance?' James asked. 'You obviously have the space, and the fine stables are no less than he deserves. I'll promise to pay you a regular rent no matter what, and if anything happens to me, Archie won't be disorientated. And you can feel free to ride him from time to time if it takes your fancy.'

Lance smiled broadly, saying without a moment's hesitation, 'You have yourself a deal, James. That's a very thoughtful act on your behalf. Not too many people would put an animal first; before their own personal feelings and self-gratification. I commend you, my friend.'

James hauled himself on to the large horse and respectfully galloped him along Watling Street, before returning like the cat that got the cream.

'He's faultless, James. You've got yourself a once-in-a-lifetime prize,' said Lance eagerly.

Henry nodded in agreement, with a contented smile and an educated eye. 'Aye, I have to say he's as good as it gets.' He agreed.

The facial expression of James Myers changed drastically from sheer contentment to grave concern. The realisation of the possibility of finding himself in the position where he couldn't financially afford his new-found best friend, coupled with the embarrassment of having to let Lance down after all his painstaking effort, weighed heavily on his mind.

'How much are you asking for him, Lance?' asked James, his body noticeably tensing with anticipation of hearing something he really didn't want to hear.

'You don't have to concern yourself with that, James. Archie is a gift from Jerry and me,' said Henry proudly. 'We promised you we would look out for you now George is no longer here for you, so this is our way of telling you we're true to our word.'

'Ah, here we go. Sit down, lads,' said Lance upon catching a glimpse of his apprentice crossing the busy street, his arms outstretched before him, carrying a box filled to the brim with ale and pies. Lance swiftly cleared his workbench of his tools to make way for the little feast that lay ahead. The three men sat down together, being joined by the young shy apprentice.

'You know something?' said James as he gulped down his ale.

'What?' replied Henry, who was far too engrossed in his food to raise his head and acknowledge his friend.

'George told me on more than one occasion, drunk and sober, of a morbid dream that kept repeating itself to him. Horrible it was. He said that in this dream his time had finally come, and he met with his comeuppance and was scragged[1] and gibbeted, but weirdly he could see himself. He was looking down on himself swinging in the wind.

'It was always in the dark of night, the moon was always full, and then this ugly old hag with a gaunt-looking silver-haired old man, stick thin with sharp features, much like herself, pulled up beside him in a cart. It was the same cart that drew him through the streets before he met his end. The old man removed his rickety old ladders from the back of the cart, placing them on the gibbet and slowly proceeded to climb up beside him, whereupon he pulled out a razor-sharp knife and cut off his right hand.

'He then descended the ladder just as slowly as he climbed it, giving the hand to the old hag who was sitting patiently on the passenger seat of the cart. She held it in a cupping fashion in both hands, staring at it gleefully and then, without warning, started laughing in an eerie shrieking manner. The man then climbed back on to the cart and they slowly trotted away, her piercing screams of laughter still to be heard as the cart trundled out of view into the night's

---

[1] Hung

darkness. He told me he thought his severed hand was to be used in witchcraft, and that his soul would never be at rest because of it.'

Lance looked at James. 'I know what that is. It's called the hand of glory. It's said to be used by witches and warlocks. I was once told a story about this by a traveller passing by whose horse had lost a shoe. The incident took place at an inn somewhere in Northumberland on one dark winter's night when the inn had just closed. There was a tap on the door, the door was opened, and there stood without, shivering and shaking, a poor beggar, his rags soaked with the rain, and his hands red raw from the cold winter wind.

'He asked piteously for a lodging and it was cheerfully granted to him. There was no spare bed in the house so he was told he could lie on the mat before the kitchen fire. He thanked them for their kindness, and everyone went to bed except for the cook, who from the back kitchen could see into the large room. She watched the beggar, and saw him, as soon as he was left alone, draw himself up from the floor, seat himself at the table and extract from his pocket a brown withered human hand, and set it upright in the candlestick. He then anointed the fingers and applied a light to them, watching as they began to flame.

'Filled with horror, the cook rushed up the back stairs and endeavoured to arouse her master and the men of the house, but all was in vain, they slept a charmed sleep. So, in despair, she hastened down again and placed herself at her post of observation. She saw the fingers of the hand flaming, but the thumb remained unlit because one person in the house was awake.

'The beggar made himself busy collecting the valuables around him into a large sack that he'd hung on the outside of a downstairs window. Having taken all that he cared for in the large room, he entered another. On this, the cook ran in and, seizing the light, tried to extinguish the flames, but this was not easy. She poured the dregs of a beer jug over them, but they blazed even brighter, so as a last resort she picked up a jug of milk and threw it over the four lambent flames, and they died at once. Uttering a loud cry, she rushed to the door of the apartment the beggar had entered and locked it. The whole family were then woken from their deep slumber, and the thief was easily secured then hanged.'

'So, the lit fingers put the house's occupants into a deep sleep. That's creepy. No wonder George feared the gibbet. He didn't want to be dismembered and lose his soul to the devil,' said James.

'That seems to be so,' said Lance pessimistically.

Henry rubbed his chin in deep thought before saying, 'At least while Caplin's men are around, our friends' bodies are safe. We'll have to move in at the first opportunity they pull away from there. If we don't move fast, the scum will have their way.'

******

Meanwhile, Jerry remained a housebound prisoner at the Bald Faced Stag Inn, awaiting the return of Henry and James, hopefully with James's new purchase. He pulled himself up from beside the warm comforting fire and climbed the stairs, avoiding the efforts of some overnighters who tried to make some small conversation with him, returning to his room.

He climbed on to his bed and thought long and hard about George Stokes. The man had become a well-deserved obsession with him, along with his son Charles and the landlord of the Old Bear Inn. He had one major mountain to climb. The thief-taker Mathew Caplin, who sat at the top of George Stokes's excessively large payroll.

He knew it would be only a matter of time before the notorious bounty hunter would be able to persuade someone from the Old Bear Inn to be chaperoned by himself and his men to spy through the windows of every inn and tavern of London like a stalking press gang, to identify and arrest those who were with George, Ned and Thomas in the Old Bear Inn on the evening of the robbery.

After all, it was common knowledge they were a close-knit group of men who didn't welcome outsiders with open arms.

Jerry was more than aware that Mathew Caplin was fishing in a very small pond, and he didn't want himself and his friends to end their lives on the gallows to the satisfaction of the Stokes family. *No! The hunted must become the hunters*, he told himself. His four arch-enemies must be dealt with in close proximity to one another and soon – very, very soon.

Jerry's deep, intense thoughts were interrupted by the sound of voices beneath his window. He sat up in his bed and flipped open his pocket watch, cussing himself for drifting off to sleep and losing track of time. He climbed out of bed and trudged over to the window. It was Henry and James, showing off James's new horse to old Ralph.

Jerry turned and made his way downstairs and out into the semi-darkness of evening to get a closer look at the gift he'd purchased for his friend.

'What do you think of him, Jerry? Isn't he something?' called James proudly as Jerry approached.

'He looked a bit lame when you trotted him in,' said Jerry. 'I noticed it from the window.'

'Aye, and he's also short-sighted and gets grouchy when he loses at cards, but apart from that, what do you think?' said James, smiling.

'He's one of the finest horses I've ever set eyes on, James, and that's the truth,' Jerry replied.

James grew two inches taller as he puffed out his chest with pride. 'He is, isn't he. He's one handsome beast.'

Henry turned to the ageing ostler. 'Take care of him, Ralph, he's in for the night. Tomorrow he'll be going back to Lance's, where his permanent stabling will be.'

'Aye, I'll get him inside and do the necessities. You boys get yourselves out of the cold,' said old Ralph, as he took over Archie's reins.

'Yes, get him inside, Ralph,' snapped Jerry, as he turned and marched sharply back towards the inn. The three men looked at one another.

'That one's feeling better, ain't he?' whispered Ralph under his breath. 'If anyone didn't realise it before, they sure as hell will soon enough.'

The Bald-Faced Stag Inn, Putney Vale
That Evening

'I THINK we should visit George's brother Samuel tomorrow,' suggested Jerry. 'He must be suffering deeply; every bit as much as ourselves…even more so. And we haven't been near or by. I'm heading over there at ten o'clock sharp tomorrow morning if anyone wishes to ride out with me. By the way, James, the money you'd saved for your horse. Do you still have it?'

James looked at Jerry with slight apprehension. 'Of course, why?'

'Good, good. Henry will explain to you. I'm going to my room. Have my supper sent up to me,' said Jerry as he left for his room.

'We told you that we would watch over you now George is no longer with us,' Henry started to explain, 'and that's exactly what we're doing, James. The horse we purchased for you is your horse, make no mistake about that. Archie will be your companion until his or your time comes to meet the reaper but, it must be said, times are changing. Things aren't like they used to be. More and more toll gates and more and more mounted lawmen have dictated that we have to move with the times. We're the last of a dying breed my friend.

'Five, maybe ten years from now our like will no longer be doing what we're doing. It will be time to look in another direction to supply our needs. But at this moment in time you must buy another working horse. Jumping Joe is taking care of that for us, and he can do the same for you if you wish, but be sure to remember you must never, ever rob or do anything untoward when you're with Archie. Is that clear?' James nodded.

'Jerry was not nosing into your business earlier,' Henry continued. 'There's good reason behind him asking you such a personal question. His subtlety seems to have abandoned him for now, but he can be forgiven, he's not been through the best of times himself. He asked about your funds because you need a

74

capital working horse, something that's nondescript, young and faster than a shot from a well-made musket. That comes at a price, and you need to top up the money you have for the horse Joe sold for you. Can you do that? And would you like Joe to take responsibility for your next horse?'

'If Joe's selecting is good enough for you and Jerry, then it's good enough for me,' James replied.

Henry grinned broadly. 'I'll take that as a yes.'

'Our Jerry was talking in his sleep last night; did you hear him, Henry?' James asked.

'Aye, I did. His mind's racing and chasing in all directions. We have too many people that need to be taken down a peg or two, and he obviously feels it should all be taken care of in an instant. And to put the cherry on the cake, we were had over by some smugglers last week. That's why he's so adamant that Joe should get your horse for you.'

'Smugglers, Henry?' asked James.

'Aye, smugglers. Three conniving bloody smugglers. Three slippery eels. Jerry and me made a grave mistake, breaking possibly every rule in the book of common sense. We did what we did because we both weren't on top form, and I let him do it because I wanted him to focus on something apart from the obvious. It was foolhardy I know, but it happened and what's done is done.'

James expelled a deep breath with a sigh. 'What bloody happened, Henry? Spit it out.'

'We made a deal with three smugglers, purchasing two bay geldings from them. Jerry wanted to close the deal but because, like I said, he was still as weak as a kitten and sickly at the time, he foolishly paid them half the money up front. The three bags of scum obviously sensed my and Jerry's fragility and took advantage of it to the full by taking our money and vanishing into thin air without upholding their end of the deal. So now you know, and I would appreciate it if what's just been said between us goes no further.'

The Home of Samuel Alston, Wimbledon
11 May 1791, 10.30 am

S AMUEL SAT despondently at his kitchen table, clasping a tankard of lukewarm ale. His eyes stared vacantly into space as if he were in a heavy hypnotic trance. His thoughts were of his brother George, and Ned and Thomas. *If only I hadn't told them of George Stokes and his property, they would still be here.*

His thoughts flashed back to the last time he'd set eyes on them, picturing them as they rode off together from his home, their smiling faces never to be erased from his memory. Never will they grow old.

He began to wonder how they would have looked in old age, what they would have been doing with their lives. Would George still have had his tavern with Jenny? Would Ned still have been overzealous with his pugilistic tendencies, challenging any young pretender that dared to cross his path? Would Thomas still have had his cheeky, sarcastic wit and dark humour that always came to light at the gravest of moments, sending all around him into fits of uncontrollable laughter? A fragmented smile broke out across his sad pale face. *Yes! They undoubtedly would have.* The sound of panting horses and talking broke him away from his sorrowful thoughts. It was Jerry, Henry and James. He stayed put, unable to muster the strength or enthusiasm to go and greet them. He could hear them talking to his wife Ann, but they were too far away for him to hear clearly. Moments later, his friends made their way towards the house, the sound of gravel crunching louder and louder under foot as they neared the kitchen door. Even this reminded him of his brother, for it was he who suggested surrounding his isolated home with a gravel path to forewarn his family of visitors.

'Hello, Samuel,' said James, making a point of being the first over the threshold. 'Is it within yourself to let us take a seat with you?'

'Of course, sit yourselves down. You're always welcome, you know that.' Henry and James pulled up a couple of stools and joined him at the table. Jerry remained standing, reaching into the side pocket of his coat and retrieving his tobacco pouch and short meerschaum pipe. He looked at the fireplace, where the fire had died some time ago. Samuel was behaving out of character. Jerry dug deeper into his pocket and retrieved the implements for striking a light. He filled his pipe, lit it and started smoking. 'Our grief isn't going to heal in life's slow natural way, Samuel, until we find closure,' Jerry said. 'George and the boys need to be laid to rest before that process can begin to take place. That bastard Stokes and his son of a bitch are deliberately restricting that process. They're not fools. They're completely aware of their actions. It's also come to my attention that Stokes and Caplin are trying to stir up public indignation at the failure of the authorities to bring us to justice.'

Jerry walked around the table, his countenance calm, his step slow and composed as he continued. 'If we sit back and continue in this manner, it will become our undoing. The clock's ticking. Their investigations have probably put us at the top of their list of suspects, but of proof we can be sure they have none. But they'll become increasingly more anxious as each day passes, and the possibility of them hauling us in one at a time for questioning can't be ignored. They'll be looking for flaws in our statements and it wouldn't take much for Mathew Caplin to twist it to his advantage.

'If they visit you, Samuel, tell them you haven't seen us for some time. Make it clear to them that you don't have anything to do with us. We were your brother's friends, not yours. Tell them you have no reason to know of our business and our whereabouts. We'll keep in touch with you, but not here anymore. There's every possibility your comings and goings will be monitored for a short time until they've satisfied themselves. If you need to contact us, leave a message with Lance Andrews.'

Samuel nodded in acknowledgment, saying, 'By the way Jerry, my employer asked me how George knew of the Stokes family home.' The three outlaws glanced at one another, sharing the same thoughts, before instinctively drawing their bodies closer to Samuel and giving him their full undivided attention.

'What was said Samuel?' asked Jerry in a quiet, almost inaudible whisper.

'I told him it was pure coincidence, and that I hadn't spoken to George for several months up until his death, due to a horrible family row that escalated out of control and now I wished we'd buried the hatchet and forgiven each other.'

'And he believed you?' asked Jerry.

'To be honest, I don't really know. I think deep down his instincts told him otherwise, but he wanted to give me the benefit of the doubt. He thinks highly of me, you see. I've never let him down in all the years I've been in his employment.'

Samuel hung his head shamefully, before adding, 'Well, up until now that is. He's always trusted me implicitly and I likewise with him, but I know I gave him the answers he wanted to hear. Although he tried his damnedest not to show it, I could clearly see it was music to his ears, and how could you blame him for that. If the boot was on the other foot, I'd be thinking the same thing.

'His fears of George's knowledge of the Stokes family home leaking to the newspapers because George's brother was in his employment, would have been the beginning of the end for his company. They don't just live off a reputation of craftsmanship and excellence, they also function on trust, discretion and honesty. That's why he's so careful with the staff he employs. I think he went against all his instincts and threw away his rule book to give me a chance in life, and I have to live with that on top of everything else. I let him down terribly and have plummeted to the depths of those loose-tongued lilies in the brothels who hand out snippets of information to the Runners in turn for a blind eye.'

Jerry removed his pipe from his mouth before asking, 'And is that how the conversation ended, Samuel?'

'No, no. He then asked me to forget that the conversation had ever taken place.'

A look of unparalleled relief ran over the three outlaws' faces. Jerry drew in the smoke yet again from his pipe before expelling the contents like a factory chimney into the small surroundings of the kitchen.

'If he ever raises the conversation again,' said Jerry, 'go to Lance Andrews and let him know immediately.'

The Talbot Inn, Southwark
22 June 1791, 4 pm

'HAVEN'T SEEN you in a while, Jerry love. I thought you'd tired of me and run off with somebody else,' said the landlady in her usual chirpy manner.

'No, Gwen. Never will I get tiresome of you my lovely. I haven't been too well, but I'm over it now. As a matter of fact, it was the thought of seeing you again that kept me from death's door.'

'Well, whatever it was you managed to survive. It hasn't taken the wind out of your sails, you silver-tongued rascal.' Jerry raised his eyebrows wryly in unison with the muffled laughter from Henry and James. He watched her pour their ales without giving a second thought to the possibility that they wanted anything different.

Jerry slumped back into his chair, his eyes musing on the well-dressed landlady. He studied her covertly as she went about her duties, a combination of amazement and fascination running through his mind, intrigued at how Father Time and such a prolific lifestyle had tried its utmost to ravage her looks and beat her down. Yet strangely, although these factors had taken their toll, she was still an exceptionally attractive and strong woman.

'I saw your friends in here the other evening, Jerry love,' said Gwen as she went about her chores.

'And who might these friends be, Gwen?' asked Jerry as he sipped at his ale.

'You know. The ones you've entertained here in the past, those scruffy vagabonds that made nuisances of themselves all evening and almost came to blows with some of the local lads.'

'What did they have to say?' asked Jerry in an uncaring manner, disguising his deep interest.

'The cheeky devils tried to sell us some smuggled brandy. I told them we don't want to get closed down, and that this is a respectable establishment. We get by perfectly well without their iffy watered-down spirits.'

Jerry smiled. 'Good for you, Gwen. You tell 'em. I wonder where they got the brandy from because those two couldn't smuggle apples out of an orchard,' he said, playing down the men as if they were a couple of fools.

'Well, they didn't exactly tell me anything, but I overheard them talking.' The eyes of Henry and James widened as they tried to stifle their laughter.

Gwen continued. 'I think it's over in Wapping somewhere. Yes, that's right…Wapping. I picked up pieces of their conversation throughout the evening. Aye, Wapping it was.'

'Not that you were listening in then, Gwen,' said James with amusement.

'Well, the more they drank the louder they became,' said Gwen defensively. 'You know how it is. Apparently, that's also where they're living at the moment, and spending most of their time in the Devil's Tavern.' Gwen hesitated for a moment, mulling over her thoughts. 'Yes, I'm sure that's where they were staying.' Nodding elegantly to herself in reassurance. 'If you ask me, they should all be right at home there. Full of smugglers, cut-throats and footpads. Oh, and I think one of them was called McAully.'

The Devil's Tavern, Wapping, London
The Same Evening, 6.30 pm

'WHAT'S THIS piece of paper?' enquired Haig McAully, as he curled his lip into a contemptuous sneer.

Jerry pointed to the head of his invoice. 'This is what you stole from us, and below is the amount you must redeem us with. Personally, I don't see any good reason why we ought to see each other again in this world, so if you don't pay what's due, I'll send you elsewhere!'

McAully smirked with an arrogance that came naturally, as his eyes shifted and flickered like those of an anxious, cornered wild animal. He knew his friends were due to arrive any time soon.

Henry recaptured his attention. He too was aware they wouldn't be alone for long. 'The harsh reality of the matter is that you stole from us. You understand we can't let that go. Now think hard and quickly about how you're going to go about repaying your debt that sits at the bottom of, as you put it, this piece of paper.'

McAully studied it carefully. It was clear he wasn't totally literate. 'I took from your hand twenty guineas. You now expect twenty-five guineas. You must understand I don't have that kind of money. What I do have is tied up with that of my friends. I can only pay you in one of two ways – tonight's incoming shipment of brandy or I can have for you tomorrow the two fine bay geldings I promised you before.'

Jerry knew he had a small window of opportunity to get the horses and take a share of the brandy. McAully's men were highly dangerous people. Jerry knew how they worked. They were a well-organised gang that landed their booty mostly by brute strength, always heavily armed with pistols and cudgels. They would line the beaches in such large numbers that preventative forces could only stand by helplessly and watch as they continued about their business.

He also knew that McAully had no intention of fulfilling his hollow worthless promise. Once he was back in the safety of his fellow smugglers they would be back where they started, full circle.

Henry pulled out his knife, pushing it hard into McAully's ribs, making him wince. 'You're coming with us now. We want to see exactly where these horses are.'

'Don't worry yourselves none, boys,' said McAully. 'The horses really do exist.'

'So, you really do have a genuine deal with this farmer, is that right, McAully?' demanded Henry.

'Aye, but of course. I told him if you decided to buy, I'd collect the horses and bring them to you, and return with his money.'

James rolled his eyes in disbelief. 'And he bloody believed you? Why are you doing this person such a favour? What's in it for you?'

'There's nothing in it as such, boys,' replied McAully. 'The farmer owns some unused cowsheds that we use from time to time to store our contraband. He gets paid for that and a little more for the risk factor. It's enough to keep his head above water because he's a bit of a lazy bastard. Had it handed down to him, you know the type.

'Same with the horses. He told me he was going to sell them, but that's all he ever did, talk about it, time and time again, so I thought I'd sell them for him and put a little bit on for myself. That way everyone would be happy, and he'd no longer give me earache about them, but when you offered to pay me half in advance…well…it was just too irresistible for an old lag like me. I had myself a nice sum of money in my pocket and didn't need to take the deal any further.'

'And maybe do the same thing to someone else. Would I be correct in thinking such a thing?' asked Henry.

'Yes. It did run through my mind. Like yourselves, I was born a scoundrel and I'll die a scoundrel, so don't look so bloody surprised.'

'You have one mighty pair of balls, McAully. I give you that,' said Jerry, pondering momentarily. 'Well you can tell your farmer friend that the deal is back on, and we're paying you on delivery of the geldings.'

'Paying on delivery?' asked the old smuggler with concern.

'Aye, we'll pay you the existing half of what we agreed on delivery, which will take place tonight,' said Jerry with a cold smile that hadn't been seen for some time. Henry and James looked at one another, grinning broadly. Jerry was back and firing with both barrels.

'But I no longer have the other half of the money, Jerry boy. It's invested in the next shipment of brandy, you know that,' said the old smuggler, hoping for a little leniency to come his way.

'We've discussed this little matter already, old timer, and realise the deal won't take place without the farmer receiving his full quota, so we'll pay the full amount, and after the deal is completed we've another plan in mind for you to restore the other half of what you owe us in the form of the brandy, with a little extra in goodwill on your behalf. Now where does this farmer reside?'

'Shoreditch. The farm sits on the outskirts of Shoreditch. It's not far, about three miles.'

'Good. Good. Let's go and close the first part of this deal of ours,' said Jerry.

Croft Farm, Shoreditch, East London
The Same Evening, 7.45 pm

'GO TELL your friend the deal is back on with the same fellows as before,' Jerry instructed McAully.

'If he tries to put you off for the evening, have none of it. Don't take no for an answer. We'll remain here, just out of view.' Jerry removed his spyglass from his pocket, before adding, 'And don't forget I'll be watching you like a hawk, so tread very carefully. Now go and collect our horses and be sure to get a bill of receipt and a signature.' McAully took the money and headed off down the track to the farmhouse, as Jerry watched his every movement.

After they had waited a while, James glimpsed at his pocket watch. 'It's eight o'clock, all but five. Where is the little bastard? You don't think he's nipped off around the back and slipped away, do you?'

'No, I don't think so,' said Jerry, his spyglass still locked between his eye and the farmhouse. 'I can still see his horse. Ah, here we go.' Jerry watched intently as the front door opened and the portly farmer emerged, followed closely by Haig McAully. Jerry watched every slow, lethargic footstep as they lumbered over to the stables, before returning with the horses to the front of the farmhouse. McAully shook hands rigorously with the farmer and made his farewells before trotting back up the track with his two new acquisitions. The three outlaws studied the geldings' movements with intense scrutiny as he approached.

'Did you get a signed bill of receipt?' asked Henry, before McAully had a chance to speak.

'I have it right here, don't worry yourselves,' said the cocky smuggler, tapping his breast pocket proudly.

'Give it to me,' demanded Jerry sternly. McAully winced with frustrated anger at the disrespect coming his way as he handed it over.

'Two bay geldings sold to your good self for forty guineas, and signed for as asked,' said the smuggler.

Jerry read through the receipt swiftly, and asked, 'What's the name of your farmer friend?'

'William Boyes,' came the reply. 'Why do you ask?'

'Because I don't trust you, and I like to reassure myself.'

The four men dug in their heels and made their way back to Southwark with their six horses.

'I suppose you boys expect me to repay you with this evening's brandy shipment?' asked McAully.

'Unless you can think of a better way to redeem yourself and cover your debts,' replied Jerry cynically.

Haig McAully smiled. 'Good, then leave it with me. Where are you boys staying the night? I'll get back to you and discuss the amount that has to be settled and arrange delivery to where you wish it to be stored.'

Henry grinned broadly. 'You just keep trying. I have to give it to you, McAully…unbelievable, fucking unbelievable!'

The men stopped a short distance from Borough High Street. Henry and Jerry looked at James. No words were spoken as he took control of the two horses' reins, and Jerry handed him the bill of receipt.

'It's time we went our separate ways,' said Jerry, as James broke away from the three men and trotted off with the geldings.

The two remaining outlaws' personalities changed instantly as their friend departed, becoming volatile and menacing. Haig McAully had never seen them in this light before, and he was startled and confused. He found them creepy. His instincts told him they weren't pretenders. He'd seen so many fraudulent men pretending to be something they weren't, but this was something he hadn't encountered in all his years. They were acting like strangers he'd just met for the first time…distant…very, very distant. All the tell-tale signs of the type of men to be avoided at all costs were there. He'd met their type before, but they were usually loners. These two together, feeding off one another instinctively, chilled him to the bone.

'If you try taking the fucking piss out of us once more…just once more, we'll torture you within an inch of your shitty, worthless fucking life, and repeat the process again and again until you beg us to fucking finish you off,' growled Jerry behind clenched teeth. He was seething with anger, his face red raw with rage, the veins in his neck protruding like thick stems of ivy on the trunk of a tree, and his fists clenched into a vice-like grip, eager to pounce upon the hapless smuggler for the slightest reason.

'You know where your brandy is stored,' said Jerry, 'and you know who'll be guarding it. You're going to take us there and remove your full quota of barrels, nothing less and nothing more. We've a cart waiting at the George Inn. You'll take it and we'll follow you. Where's it stored?'

'Cheapside. It's in a lock-up in Cheapside. There are no guards. It would be too obvious and would arouse the suspicions of the authorities. It's under lock and key behind two large strong doors.'

'Who has the fucking key?' demanded Jerry.

McAully lifted his leg, revealing a small purpose-built pocket on the side of his boot. 'Four of us have a key each,' he said.

Henry stared at his boot, quietly impressed with his ingenuity. 'Well, we only need one, old man, to get us through that door, and yours will do,' he said.

The Bald-Faced Stag Inn, Putney Vale
30 June 1791, 8.30 am

JERRY GAZED outside from the downstairs room. It was a fine clear morning; the sky was as blue as blue could be and a dew-covered cobweb glistened like a princess's necklace in the corner of the window as he eyed a light vapour of mist hovering under the trees and hedgerows. A robin red breast sat on a fence post opposite, momentarily making eye contact with him, before dashing off about its business. *It's going to be a fine day*, he thought to himself, whilst taking a sip of his coffee.

His little moment of tranquillity was broken by the familiar sound of the adjoining door to the stables creaking open sharply. It was James Myers, who was carrying an expression on his face that told Jerry that he had something worth telling.

'You're early, James,' said Jerry quietly as he moved away from the window and placed himself down at a table that harboured his awaiting newspaper.

James's eyes flickered around the room checking for unwanted ears before he spoke. 'Lance has just been in touch and gave me a message for you. He's just seen Jenny. She was getting into a post-chaise outside St Paul's. She was wearing a bonnet, but he still recognised her. He was exercising my horse Archie at the time and followed the chaise to talk to her but thought better of it. He said she didn't look approachable. She made her way to the home of George's Aunt Agnes in Farringdon. He said he couldn't hang around any longer due to some noisy street hawkers making themselves busy and he didn't want to draw attention to himself.'

'At George's Aunt Agnes's, you say?' asked Jerry as he climbed from his chair. 'Stay here, James, I'll take your horse. Mine isn't saddled. I must find out how she's keeping.'

******

A short time later, Jerry was in Farringdon, gingerly knocking the door of George's Aunt Agnes, hoping that Jenny's response to him wouldn't be hostile. He braced himself for a possible onslaught of blame and accusations. The door was opened by a slim silver-haired woman who immediately recognised the visitor.

'Oh, Jerry. How are you dear? Come in,' said Agnes, beckoning Jerry in.

'How are you, Agnes? Are you keeping your chin up?' Jerry pecked her affectionately on the cheek before making his way through to the living room. As he reached the door, he noticed the lone figure of a woman sitting on a chair in the corner of the kitchen, wearing a bonnet and trying her utmost to conceal herself.

'Hello, Jenny,' Jerry greeted the woman. 'Hello, Jerry.'

'You're not about to leave, are you?' he asked, hoping that was not the case.

'No, not yet,' came Jenny's whispered reply.

'She's been here some time, and she won't take off her coat and bonnet,' said Agnes, hoping that if Jenny did, she would stay a little longer.

Jerry looked at the woman who had had such an impact on his close friend. Stokes had destroyed her emotionally as well as physically. The beautiful, kind, level-headed woman looked stick thin. Her wonderful eyes that always told you she was high on life were now cold, empty and expressionless. It was clear for all to see that she was missing George badly and that her mind was incapable of adjusting to his passing.

'Jenny, can we go for a short walk?' Jerry asked. 'I'd like to talk to you. I hope you don't think I'm being rude, Agnes.'

'No, love, don't you mind me. You'll come back though, won't you?'

'Of course. We won't be long,' said Jerry with a reassuring smile.

Jenny pulled herself up from the chair. She looked lethargic and frail for one so young. Jerry took her arm as they walked steadily down the street.

'Jenny, we're going to kill George Stokes and his son for what they did,' Jerry told her. 'And once we've done that, we're going to lay George and the boys to rest. Once the Stokes's are out of the picture, Caplin will no longer have the funds or the interest to continue watching over them.'

Jenny's face remained expressionless at the words that had just passed between Jerry's lips, as she continued walking.

'You'd better get busy and cut down my George and the boys and find a nice spot to lay them to rest,' said Jenny. 'I'd like my George to be buried across from the Green Man. That was where we first met, so I think that would be fitting. It doesn't have to be marked in any way. I'll only visit it the once to say my goodbyes. My memories are all up here.' Jenny added, as she touched her bonnet gently.

'As soon as the Stokes's are dealt with, I'll personally take care of your wishes Jenny, I promise you.'

Jenny looked up at Jerry, making eye contact for the first time, as she spoke. 'The Stokes's have already been taken care of Jerry. You'd better go and bring the boys home.'

Jerry stopped in his tracks and turned towards her, unclear whether he'd heard her quietly spoken words correctly. 'What do you mean, Jenny? Already taken care of?'

'I put the two surly bastards to sleep yesterday evening as they made their way to their local. I decided to go down there to watch their movements in order to get revenge and got lucky I suppose, because the first night I was there, I crossed their path as they were walking into the Old Bear Inn. If I'd been there a minute earlier, I'd have missed them. It was at that moment right there that a strange thing happened to me. I slipped into some kind of a trance I suppose. It's the only way I can explain it. A white light appeared up in the corner of my right eye, and there before me was an image of George. Only his head and shoulders were visible. He looked immaculate and at ease. He smiled and then faded away.

'I turned and rode away, feeling sick, as if all the energy had been sucked out of me. By the time I returned to my lodgings I felt awful and it took quite some time to recover from the experience, I can tell you. But as I slowly recovered, I was left with some knowledge that I can't explain away to you.

'It was a Thursday evening when all of this took place, but I knew they would be returning back there on the Friday at the exact same time. I just knew. There was no doubt whatsoever in my mind. It was George…he told me. I felt much comfort from that Jerry. I also knew that when I returned the next day, I'd be safe.

'I returned the following evening at the exact same time to the minute, and low and behold there they were. They had been drinking more than their share before they had reached the Old Bear, because they were as bowsie as could be. I stopped a short distance from the inn and stared at them. They noticed me and approached me, arrogantly asking if I had a problem with them. I was dressed as a man you see.

'As they closed in on me, they both peered through the darkness to get a better look. I kept my focus on George Stokes as they neared, glaring into his eyes, for my own benefit rather than anything else. I think I was hoping to see a man haunted by his own conscience, but all I saw was a man who was consumed with alcohol far more than he should have been. Needless to say, it wasn't what I'd hoped for. I still can't believe I thought such a ridiculous thing…a bastard is a bastard. Nothing in the world is going to change that.

'It was at that point I pulled the trigger and then turned my other pistol on that deplorable son of his. I then took their purses and watches to make it look like a robbery, to hopefully blind the law's eyes of suspicion. I then rode back to where I'd hidden my chaise, attached my horse and changed my clothes back to those of a respectable lady and hoped for the best.'

'Luck undoubtedly seemed to be on your side, Jenny,' said Jerry, looking at her with a new-found respect.

'It wasn't luck, Jerry. George was riding beside me last night. I knew I wasn't going to come to any harm. Do you know, Jerry? I shot the rats with George's own pistols. If you're going to seek revenge, do it properly.'

'I didn't know you were familiar with firearms, Jenny.'

'George taught me how to shoot. He said it might come in useful one day.'

Jerry raised his eyebrows in astonishment. 'He wasn't bloody wrong, was he,' he said with a smile.

The pair walked on in silence for a few moments before Jerry grinned to himself.

'What's so amusing, Jerry?' quizzed Jenny, curious. 'The watches you took from the Stokes's. They hadn't had them five minutes. They were replacements for the ones we stole from them.'

'I know. I'm wondering whether you could bury them with George.'

Jerry smiled and nodded his head in approval. 'Nice touch, Jenny, nice touch.'

******

Tears trickled freely down the face of James Myers as the cold unforgiving wind beat repeatedly against his solemn young face, making his eyes sting and squint, yet another of life's little contributions to his never-ending pain.

Jerry pulled his mask up over his face in the same habitual manner as when carrying out a robbery on some unsuspecting soul, but this time it was for a different reason, not to take what wasn't his, but to steal back the bodies of his departed friends and quell the despicable stench of rotting, infested flesh.

James and Henry followed likewise. Henry peered at James from under his tightly pulled down hat, his mask failing miserably to conceal his distorted expressions of sorrow. The three men slowed to an apprehensive stop, looking to assess the task in front of them, as the chains clanked eerily against the damp cold timbers of the creaking gibbets. James let out a sharp whine.

'Your mind and body must remain strong, my friend,' Henry told James. 'We've a job that needs finishing. Our brothers need to be laid to rest and it's going to be done right now.'

James immediately took stock of himself, obeying his friend's stern rasping words as he looked incessantly at Henry's masked face. He'd seen the vision on numerous occasions before as they robbed and plundered up and down the king's highway, but this time things were different. He didn't look the same. Never before had he witnessed such a look of pure intense determination. If Henry was fighting with his inner emotions, they weren't apparent. His mind was set on the job in hand.

They set about the task of cutting down the caged bodies, and as undignified as it looked, proceeded to drag them behind their horses into the seclusion of the nearby woodland, before placing them into an awaiting wagon under the safe protection of Jumping Joe. Covered in blankets, their friends were finally escorted to their places of eternal rest.

Police Office, Union Hall, London
2 July 1791

THE FAMOUS Bow Street Runner John Townsend marched sure-footedly towards his office door. He was a short stout straight-talking man with a flaxen wig, kerseymere breeches, a blue straight-cut coat and a broad-brimmed hat; a man who never minced his words and didn't suffer fools.

Mathew Caplin was waiting for him outside his office door. He acknowledged his visitor with a nod as he turned his key and made his way inside. Caplin followed.

'So, tell me, Mr Caplin, what exactly is of such great importance for you to ask to meet with me at such short notice?'

Townsend's abrupt words made his feelings towards the man all too clear. A man whose business he referred to as a rabble of conspiring scoundrels with a very suspect ideology on how law and order should be enforced, particularly when bringing to justice the poorer and weaker elements of society.

'Mr Townsend, since the murders of George Stokes and his son Charles, the corpses of George Alston, Edward Simpson and Thomas Ledbury have been stolen from their gibbets the very moment we terminated our watch over them,' Caplan explained before continuing. 'I'm aware that Lewis Jeremiah Avershaw and his gang were at the George Inn, Southwark at the time of the murders with as many as twenty witnesses to verify that fact. I'm also aware, as you know, that two of your officers were also drinking in the very same establishment at the time and are witness to that fact. With that said, I still believe that Avershaw and his men are responsible for the stealing of their friends' bodies from their gibbets on Wimbledon Common.'

'I agree with you entirely, sir. We're of the same mind on this matter, but we don't have the time and resources to run around chasing shadows. Do you have any information to put to me whereupon we can gather substantial evidence regarding the matter? Or is it pure assumption at this point in time? Let me make myself perfectly clear to you, sir. We're a professional police force that works on hard factual evidence, not hearsay and gossip.

'If, sir, you have hard proof or anything as such to give us a lead and a strong possibility of bringing about the apprehension of these culprits, it will be well received. But the fact is that Stokes and his son were killed, and their purses and valuables taken, and Avershaw and his associates were at the George Inn, Southwark at the time. This doesn't make good for arresting them. It could well be that other parties were involved. So, unless you have anything else to tell me, I wish you good day, sir!'

The Green Man Inn, Putney Heath
3 September 1791

'I'M GOING back to Carlisle to live with my family now that I've taken care of what I came back here to do,' Jenny informed Jerry, as they walked outside the inn. 'There's nothing to keep me here anymore…not now George has gone. Before we met, I was thinking of going back, but then he walked into my life and that all changed.'

Jenny smiled at the thought of their first meeting. 'When he walked up to the bar, you could tell by the looks on the other men's faces that he wasn't a man to be messed with, but when he spoke to me for the first time he behaved like a shy little boy. He would fumble his words, and to tell you the truth, I was much the same with him. Sounds silly doesn't it, two grown adults acting that way, but that was the way it was. He'd sit down with you all, but craftily kept his cheeky eyes on me at every opportunity, and of course I noticed it because I was doing exactly the same to him.'

Jerry broke into a cheeky smile. 'I know, Jenny. We all noticed how you were with each other. The pair of you weren't that crafty. To tell you the truth we were all a little envious of what you had.'

'Well, you don't have to be envious anymore. Oh, I miss him so much. What am I going to do?'

Jerry placed his arm around her in a vain attempt to comfort her as best he could. 'He'll always be around you, Jenny. His spirit will never die. You just have to learn to be able to tune into the little things that let you know his presence is around and watching over you as best he can.'

Jenny looked down at the grave beneath the old oak tree, not far from the inn. 'We can't even give him a headstone, bless him,' she said sadly. She frustratingly dabbed away a tear with her handkerchief as Jerry took her by the arm and led her closer to the ageing oak.

Jenny smiled and then cried as she read the words carved within a scroll: *Here lies in dust Big George Alston, never to be forgotten.* 'That's the finest headstone you're ever going to see. I think George would have liked it.'

A heavy freak wind stirred up from nowhere, shaking every branch of the big imposing oak, before drifting back to tranquillity as quickly as it had arrived.

Jerry looked up through glazed eyes and gave a knowing smile. 'It looks like he does.'

Jenny turned and took one last look at the inn that had spawned so many wonderful dreams, knowing she would never return, and that this chapter in her life was now forever closed.

Hereford, England
14 October 1791

SIR GILES Beucroft and his trusted butler were preparing for their trip to London. 'How's your son getting on, Ferguson?' asked Sir Giles as he poured himself a small glass of port. His words of concern towards his butler were justified, as Ferguson had only the fortnight before buried his wife Florence, and their only child Richard had drawn deep into himself, disorientated with life after losing the woman who was his guiding light.

Young Richard had worshipped her as much as she did him, and now she had been snatched from him and his father by forces beyond their control. Sir Giles was also aware that Richard was drifting towards further troubled waters with a small group of local boys, and felt a certain sense of responsibility towards the youngster, both because his loyal butler hadn't been given the opportunity to fulfil his duties as a father because of their many extensive business trips to London and Bath during the essential years of young Richard's life and because he genuinely cared.

'Unfortunately, I'm having some difficulties with him, sir,' replied Ferguson. 'I feel it's time for him to find steady employment now he's finished school. I hope you don't mind my asking, and I do hope you don't think it impertinent of me, but I was wondering if at any time a vacancy arises within the household, you might possibly give him some consideration? I ask because I believe that it wouldn't take long in such a well-disciplined environment for him to iron out his minor shortcomings and get himself back on the straight and narrow once again. I feel that all he needs is pointing in the right direction, because he's such an intelligent and engaging young man.'

Sir Giles smiled. His intuition as always had served him well. His loyal butler's words were half expected. The many years Ferguson had spent in his service had taught Sir Giles how to read him like a book.

'I've spoken to Osgood, our coachman, and he tells me we're in need of a new stable boy,' said Sir Giles. 'Apparently the young chap didn't know when to hold his tongue, and although he was warned on several occasions, he hadn't made the slightest attempt to curb his ways. So here we are looking for a new stable boy.'

'Your kindness as always overwhelms me, sir,' said the butler. 'I do believe I'll sleep far better tonight than I have done for some time. My concerns for Richard have led to much anxiety of late. I suppose when the wind is blowing against you, the further you get down the road, the more tiresome it becomes. Thanks to you, I believe I've just turned the corner and found some sanctuary. You know, sir, Richard has always had a fascination with horses, ever since he was a child. I think he'll be in his element here and it just might be the tonic to help him get over the loss of his mother. Has a time and date been established for him to make a start?'

Sir Giles took a cheerful sip of his port. 'Have a word with Richard before we leave, and if he accepts the going rate and what the job entails, he can present himself to Mr Osgood first thing Saturday morning, eight o'clock sharp.' When Richard was told of the vacancy by his father, he couldn't believe his good fortune. His night was a restless one to say the least. There was excitement entwined with apprehension. He already knew most of the staff in the household, especially in the kitchen, but the coach house and the stables were off limits. He'd seen Mr Osgood many times before, but only in passing. He always thought him to be of the mind that little boys should be seen and not heard. Richard just hoped Osgood wasn't one of those overbearing authoritarians who played god in his own little bubble. *No, no, of course not*, he told himself. *My father wouldn't place me in such a vulnerable position, especially at this moment in time. Stop over-thinking things.*

Hereford
The Following Morning

'WELL RICHARD, you're early rather than punctual, and that's better than being late. You've started off how you intend to carry on I hope.' Mr Osgood tucked in his chin and gave Richard a no-nonsense sideways look but, for all the posturing, the stern man's eyes gave Richard more than a glint of hope that he was ready to give him a fighting chance.

'Yes, Mr Osgood, sir,' said Richard with a smile as he pulled out his pocket watch and tilted it in the stout coachman's direction. 'It's with me at all times and I never forget to wind it.' Mr Osgood shared a smile. It was exactly what he wanted to hear.

******

As the days turned into weeks, and the weeks into months, it was clear that Mr Osgood had warmed to his new stable boy. He found him to be a smart and active young man, with a larger-than-life affection for the horses around him, so much so that anyone could be forgiven for thinking they were his very own.

Richard's progress bounded from strength to strength, and he never missed an opportunity to ask a question and learn more about the wonderful creatures that fascinated him so. He'd found a pathway in life. Where it would actually take him, he wasn't quite sure, but one thing he was certain of was that horses were to be a big part of it.

The year of 1792 passed quickly for Richard. Things were steady in his life, his long hours of service combined with his riding lessons helping to reduce his time with the local boys and giving him time for some much-n e e d e d personal reflection, but unbeknown to him things were about to change…and change quickly.

Richard's father took it upon himself to break the news to his son that a move to London for the household was imminent and explained the reasons behind the decision before it became common knowledge. He thought it best to explain the reasons why, where and when, and the benefits it would entail, rather than Richard being told along with everyone else employed within the stable by the word of Mr Osgood before being commissioned to the house to be given a full detailed explanation by Sir Giles and Lady Beucroft. Many of the staff understandably declined the offer and decided to look for new employment within their local community rather than make the distant move, but Richard embraced the adventure, as did his ageing father, who looked upon it with the attitude of "a change is as good as a rest".

Richard and his father helped with the move and settled quickly into their new environment with refreshed optimism. Only two weeks had passed when Richard was approached by Mr Osgood in the stables.

'Richard,' called Mr Osgood as he entered the quiet of the stables. 'Our postilion has gone down with sickness and it seems he won't be able to fulfil his duties for a while, so it's down to you to fill his boots until he recovers.'

'Yes, Mr Osgood,' came the calm, collected reply. 'You'd better go and get yourself fitted with your new rags and boots. We can't have you out and about with Lady Beucroft in that attire,' said the coachman as he turned and marched expressionlessly out of the door.

'Don't you go getting any ideas above yourself, it's not permanent you know,' said Oweyn the ostler, his tone and words portraying his unhappiness with the situation.

'Maybe, Oweyn, maybe, but they'll see what I can do won't they, and that can't be a bad thing, can it now,' replied Richard as he hastily removed his apron, pleased with the opportunity to show off the riding skills he'd acquired from his lessons.

The ostler cracked a half-hearted smile. 'That's true, young 'un, I can't begrudge you that I suppose. Don't you go taking my harsh words to heart. I'm just a little peeved at the prospect of having to take on your workload on top of my own while you're out and about.'

'Well, as you said, Oweyn, it's not permanent. It may only be for a day or two.'

However, three weeks had passed before Mr Osgood broke the predictably unwanted news. 'Arthur will be resuming his position first thing tomorrow morning, Richard. Take your uniform back to Mrs Wicks and return to your duties in the stables. You did well lad, and it hasn't gone unnoticed.'

After returning to his duties as a stable boy, it soon became apparent to Richard that he could no longer continue with a job he now deemed a lowly position, so he soon made the decision to seek employment for a postilion vacancy. His father had been away but was due to return later that very evening, so Richard took it upon himself to wait for his return and relay his thoughts on the matter. A sense of pure unadulterated relief poured over him when he found his father to be philosophical about his plans. Richard's worries of his father finding his actions ungrateful were unfounded.

'I'll miss you being around, Richard, but you're trying to better yourself, and not a person worth their salt would knock you for that,' his father assured him.

It didn't take long before Richard's hopes were fulfilled. Good fortune was on his side, and his father's good name and influence had swung it for him yet again. Lady Dunhill was a close and significant friend of the Beucrofts and had spoken to Sir Giles, asking what had become of the smart new postilion who had been replaced by the old hand. Sir Giles had explained the circumstances that dictated Richard's return to his former duties as a stable boy and of his recent wish to better himself at the first opportunity that a vacancy for a postilion arose.

'Would you have difficulty in finding another suitable stableboy, Giles, if I gave him that opportunity to better himself?' enquired Lady Dunhill.

Sir Giles smiled. 'No, not at all, Lady Dunhill. Stableboys are ten a penny, a good postilion less so. Would you like me to send for him, so you can offer him the position?'

Lady Dunhill smiled back at Sir Giles. 'Why not, there's no time like the present.'

Richard was hired instantly and thanked Lady Dunhill and Sir Giles for their kindness and understanding before returning to his work in the stables. That evening he made his way over to his father's quarters to thank him for his behind-the-scenes contribution. Ferguson's joy for his son's new opportunity was more than apparent, although Richard's erratic wayward tendencies still raised concerns with him. For one reason or another his son always seemed to be one step away from self-destruction. Ferguson was baffled about where Richard's wild line of thought derived from. It certainly wasn't from him or his wonderful Florence.

'Listen to my words, Richard.' The butler instructed his son. 'They're based on sound experience from life. When you begin your employment with Lady Dunhill, always remember to conduct yourself as a gentleman at all times because the repercussions of your actions can have a devastating effect. It doesn't begin and end with yourself alone.'

Richard's move stood him in high spirits. As 1793 went by, things couldn't have progressed better for him. He was without exception found to be a popular new addition within the household and, it would be fair to say, more so amongst the fairer sex within the household, who warmed to him at an instant, tickled by his unusual aristocratic mannerisms and quickfire humour.

But, alas, it was to be short lived. A moment of loose integrity led to him letting himself and his guarantors down badly. Richard was caught, in the words of Lord Dunhill, "in an improper situation with one of the female servants". His employment was terminated forthwith. It seemed that his father's unparalleled advice carried a short shelf life with the young man, whose moral character frailties seemed to border precariously close to those of an alley cat. A short period of time had passed before Richard found further employment at a local coach house. His aristocratic ways and skilful manipulation of the truth in order to enhance his chances of employment weren't needed, as his service within the household of Lord Dunhill was more than enough to satisfy his new employers without further investigation.

However, as the months slowly drifted by, Richard became more and more restless. The reality of working for a coach house within the city and employment within the household of Lord Dunhill bore not even a hint of comparison to his current employment. In fact, they were without question worlds apart, so much so that it depressed him to the point of taking refuge in a nearby alehouse at any God-given opportunity.

It was during this uneventful period of his life in the autumn of 1793 that Richard decided, with much apprehension, to visit his father. He hoped to enter around the back of the house in order to avoid the wrath of Sir Giles or any uncomfortable confrontation with anyone else in the house that he may happen upon, but luck wasn't on his side. He was confronted with Mr Osgood.

'Hello, Richard. The master's in the parlour. Go through, he's been trying to find you,' Osgood informed him.

Richard mumbled sombrely and with apprehension, 'Is everything alright, Mr Osgood?'

'No, lad. Go and see the master. He'll not be sharp with you. Off you go now.' Richard walked tentatively through the house and knocked on the parlour door.

'Enter,' came the stifled solitary word. Richard opened the door to see Sir Giles pacing the room with his hands behind his back, whilst Lady Beucroft remained seated, clasping a handkerchief.

'Hello, Richard. How did you learn of your father so quickly?' Sir Giles said. 'We were in the process of trying to locate you to break the awful news.'

Richard began to perspire. He felt hot and yet, at the same time, cold. 'What awful news, sir?' he asked, as an excruciating sense of helplessness flushed over his taut slim frame.

'Your father passed away in the early hours of this morning. We're so sorry. Our condolences go out to you.' Sir Giles's sadness looked genuine.

'How did he die?' asked Richard, his head beginning to feel woozy, his body as light as a feather, as if floating in its own paranormal state. His eyes locked on to those of Sir Giles.

'He was always the first to rise and take care of the servants' duties for the day,' Sir Giles explained. 'His unusual absence prompted Mrs Reeves to call for Mr Osgood. When he entered your father's room, he found him in his bed. He'd passed away in his sleep, God bless him.'

Richard looked at Sir Giles, who seemed to be ageing before his very eyes. His skin was a ghostly grey and he looked haggard. *You really did care*, Richard thought to himself, as he studied the man who referred to his father as his shadow.

The funeral was one of grand expenditure. Sir Giles and Lady Beucroft gave their butler and friend the finest of send-offs, far beyond the expectations of all that attended. The wake was catered for in exactly the same tasteful manner, with the entire household being treated to the extravagance of being waited upon, an oddity most of them would never experience again in their lifetime.

As the sad proceedings drew to a close, Richard was summoned back to the house by Sir Giles and Lady Beucroft.

'Please be seated, Richard,' said Sir Giles, telling rather than asking. 'Your father was a fine man. He was also a man of great integrity and conviction,' he continued, as he paced the full length of the room with a posture akin to that of a highland stag, trying his utmost to disguise the immeasurable sadness that lay within. 'He had an uncanny knowledge of what made the wheels of life go around, far beyond the boundaries of many of his superiors. I can tell you with the utmost sincerity that he worked hard, way beyond the call of duty for this family. I'm also very grateful that his endless support and advice to myself did, on many an occasion, help to steer my family's finances back in the right direction.'

Sir Giles paused for a moment before continuing. 'You let your father down badly, Richard. All of the staff were aware of the embarrassing predicament you placed your father in. It affected him to the extent that he took it upon himself to emphatically apologise on behalf of you and for his misguided judgement for want of bettering the life of his own flesh and blood, not to mention our own personal embarrassment.

'With that aside, we're aware of the fact that you're now alone in life, and Lady Beucroft and myself made a solemn promise to your father after your mother's passing that if anything should happen to him, we would take the necessary steps to secure a roof over your head. So, if I'm correct in thinking that you're remorseful for your moment of weakness, we'll leave the door open to you should you wish to return to continue your work within the stables.'

'Thank you, Sir Giles,' replied Richard. 'I appreciate your generous words. They're very comforting to me, but I already have employment as a postilion. You can rest with peace of mind that your generous promise to my father has been fulfilled.'

Sir Giles smiled and nodded in acceptance of Richard's words before walking over to his desk and unlocking one of its drawers, opening it and removing a small highly polished mahogany box, which had its own key in situ. He turned the key and lifted the lid.

'This box and its contents belonged to your father, Richard,' explained Sir Giles. 'We removed it from his room for safe keeping. The rest of his belongings are still there, under lock and key of course. You may collect them when you feel up to the task, but you may take this with you today if you feel that your lodgings are secure.'

Sir Giles handed over the box. 'It contains your parents' wedding rings, your father's watches and other personal items, which I'm sure you'll recognise,' Sir

Giles informed Richard, who placed the box on his lap, looking at it, observing its fine craftsmanship and pristine condition.

The box summed his father up to a tee. Richard knew that his father would have no less an item securing the treasures of his life that meant so much to him. His eyes moistened and clouded over. He quickly dabbed away a stray tear, eliminating any chance of it trespassing on to his cheek in view of Sir and Lady Beucroft.

Sir Giles led Richard over to a table on which stood a small strongbox. He ceremoniously opened it, removing a sealed letter that was resting upon a large sum of money and handed it to Richard to read.

'Your father bequeathed you his small fortune, which you'll find within the will,' said Sir Giles. 'It amounts to fifty-seven guineas. I personally will take care of the legal process in order to transfer the money to you as soon as possible. I suggested to your father some time ago that it might be a good idea to place such a significant sum into the care of the very same bank that I use, Thomas Coutts & Co., but he refrained and kept it within his strongbox. I was aware that he was placing a little away each time he received his salary, specifically for the intention of supporting you through life when the inevitable came and he would no longer be here for you.'

'I had no idea my father had done such a thoughtful thing, sir, but it doesn't surprise me.'

Sir Giles nodded. 'His thoughts were always focused on you, Richard. He was a good man and a fine butler. No, no, I retract my words. He was the best of the best.'

Richard thanked Sir and Lady Beucroft, expressing his highest appreciation for their kindness and generosity of untold expense.

'It was the least we could do,' Sir Giles assured him. 'He deserved a good send-off, and we sure as hell made sure he got one.'

By the time Richard set off on his journey back to his lodgings it was early evening. His mind was drifting back to his childhood, reminiscing about the happy times he shared with his mother and father, as he trotted his horse slowly into the darkness of a cluster of oak trees. His attention was drawn towards the sky by a small flock or raucous cawing rooks, buzzing aggressively around a lone heron as it flew graciously unperturbed from the antics of the pestering crows. It didn't change its line of direction, as hard as the rooks tried.

I wonder where you're heading, Richard thought to himself. *Are you flying to the first place you see your next meal, ending up who knows where? Then again, maybe not. Perhaps you know exactly where you're going. You have a destination.*

He compared the elegant bird's situation with that of his own. *Yes, life needs a direction just like that lone heron, pushing aside life's obstacles that consistently get in your way.* Richard had witnessed a small learning curve through a window of nature. He made up his mind at that moment, one way or another, that he was never going to be dominated or pushed around, and for certain he was never going to go without.

Shortly afterwards, Richard's much-awaited inheritance came into his possession, and it wasn't long before a new wardrobe of clothes was purchased. Stepping out one evening in his new attire, he decided to go to Thaives coffee house before heading on to the theatre. As he did so, he passed by the many inns of chancery, whereupon he witnessed four stoutly built lawyers in an overladen cart. The horse was exhausted to the point of near collapse, struggling under the strain of the overweight men. It riled him as he watched the torment of the poor animal, and all because the four lawyers were to penny-pinching to hire two carts. They were totally insensitive to the suffering they were causing the poor creature. For all their education, and all their day-to-day experiences within the courts of law, they still couldn't see any further than the depth of their pockets.

Richard stood for a moment, eyeing the men with a contemptible sneer, wondering how men of such intellect and knowledge could fall so short of obvious common sense, just for the sake of such of a paltry amount of money.

The New Drury Lane Theatre, London
2 January 1794

A S RICHARD Ferguson approached his seat, his eyes widened, and a smile was returned to an exceptionally pretty woman occupying the seat beside him. Oddly, she was alone, but it wasn't without good reason, for she was a high-class courtesan from St George's Fields called Nancy. Unbeknown to Richard, the woman that momentarily drew his gaze was to hold considerable influence over the direction of his future.

The path of the lone heron that Richard had watched had, for the time being at least, slipped his young precarious mind as he took it upon himself to ask whether he could escort the woman back to her residence. The smartly dressed young man's hopes and desires were predictably well received, with the disclosure of an over-rehearsed coy smile and nod of acceptance, which resulted in a long sleepless night that ended the following morning with the eager-to-impress young Richard parting with a gift of money far beyond his weekly earning capacity. It was clear that his life was beginning to spiral out of control, and his inheritance wasn't going to be spent in the same respectful manner as it had been earned. He pecked Nancy on the forehead with the eager promise of repeating his visit to her in the not-too-distant future.

True to his word, Richard returned to Nancy within the week, like a moth drawn to the warm bright glow of a lantern that had entered the dark evening air. His excuses to his newly found drinking companions were simple: he had to work all the hours god sends to cover a host of neglected debts, but the truth be known, he was concerned that any distance of time may mellow Nancy's memory of him, and that would be inconceivable. The sooner he had her back in his life the better, he repeatedly told himself, even though his muddled emotions often told him that he couldn't continue down this reckless, unforgiving path of self-destruction. The drinking well would indeed soon enough run dry and bring his little party to an abrupt, regrettable end.

His line of thought had without question become blurred and his self-confidence had petered to an all-time low, believing himself to be an intruder in a society to which he didn't belong. But for all this, he knew he could still maintain his deception over Nancy, who believed the impeccably dressed young man to be of considerable wealth and properties.

Unfortunately for Richard, the naivety of his ways with such a woman failed to allow him to grasp the full understanding of how the mesmerising young beauty's mind actually ticked. She would receive him with every mark of endearment in her power, for Nancy was as complete a mistress in the art of wheedling as one could find, and at this moment in time, whilst Richard was becoming acquainted with her, he was unaware that she was the favourite of several noted highwaymen, who in turn all had their favoured hours. While these rogues could supply the wealth to indulge her in every luxury and extravagance desired, she would declare to them that no other man on earth shared her loving affections.

The highwaymen of course took her words of loving sincerity with a large pinch of salt but, unfortunately for Richard, this wasn't so in his case. All of his self-imposed promises to never be taken advantage of fell heavily on stony ground as he became as big a dupe as ever she'd ensnared. His father's savings were dwindling away fast, and as the next two months drifted by, his fear of being disregarded by her weighed heavily on his mind.

In his turmoil, he continued with his overtime as a postilion to enable himself to sustain his pretence to Nancy. His hard-earned wages swiftly moved from his well-tailored pocket to the pretty courtesan's well-tailored silk purse.

The Great North Road,
Clerkenwell, London
25 March 1794

A HARSH, bitter March wind tore through the naked dancing trees, cutting unmercifully into the face of Richard Ferguson as he transported his passenger to his favoured hostelry. Richard didn't mind the weather, as his spirits were high because he was going to see Nancy that evening and take her to the theatre in Piccadilly.

Suddenly, without warning, his endearing thoughts were broken as two masked men on horseback appeared from within the dark secluded confines of a derelict windmill, the finest days of which had a long time past.

'Damn your eyes, boy, stop!' barked one of the men, who was subtly dressed, like his accomplice, in a slate-grey greatcoat, black hat and boots, his pistol cocked and aimed in the direction of Richard's stunned face.

Richard felt an uneasy nervousness. He'd never encountered the unwanted attention of high tobymen before, even though he knew there was always half a chance he would. The highwayman who had stopped him stayed close, focused like a polecat ready to pounce at the first attempt of heroism, while his over-aggressive partner in crime removed the terror-stricken passenger of his belongings. No threats, no curses, not one single word was exchanged as the accomplice stared with menace.

Richard studied the highwayman's steed, watching the way it conducted itself next to that of his own. *You've done this a hundred times before*, he told himself. *These men are veterans.*

Without warning, the wind raged harder than before, blowing the crepe from the outlaw's face, momentarily giving Richard full view of him. They stared uneasily at one another, but before a single word was exchanged, the high tobys were disturbed by the sound of approaching company, forcing them to take their leave.

Sometimes in life we see things we rather we hadn't. That fleeting moment when you wished you could turn back the hands of time just that odd couple of seconds or so, but alas you know you can't. That unfortunate moment between Richard and the highwayman was one such occasion, for he'd seen the man who held him at his mercy before. He'd met with his acquaintance and passed the odd piece of small talk with him at Nancy's. His name was Lewis Jeremiah Avershaw, known as Jerry. Richard felt a deep nauseous feeling deep down in the pit of his stomach, fully aware that this wasn't going to be the end of that short ugly encounter beside the tumbledown windmill.

Meanwhile, Jerry Avershaw was fraught with a sense of uneasiness as he spoke to Henry Watts. 'I've seen that postilion before, on more than one occasion at Nancy's. He recognised me immediately when the wind unmasked my face.'

Henry Watts listened with concern, replying, 'We can catch up with him at the Swan Inn when he makes his return. He'll water his horses there. They always do.'

The outlaws galloped with haste to the Swan Inn, placing themselves by a window in full view of the watering troughs, anxiously awaiting the arrival of the man who had seen far more than was good for him. Within the hour, Jerry's inner turmoil turned to relief, as a two-horse-drawn post-chaise pulled up alongside their window. The outlaws instantly dispatched a waiter to approach the jittery postilion and invite him to join them. Richard apprehensively agreed and made his way inside. The high tobys raised themselves from their chairs and invited him to sit with them, their gruff, harsh London accents simmering with passive intimidation beneath crocodile smiles.

Jerry picked up the conversation. 'We know each other and don't want to fall out over what's gone down here today, now do we. Have you spoken to anyone about our little encounter earlier? Think hard, think fast and think logically…you know it's in your best interest.' A veiled threat sprinkled with intimidation if ever Richard had heard one.

'No, no, I haven't told a soul,' Richard replied. 'And the gent you just robbed is crying into a complimentary brandy whilst bending the hostelry keeper's ear more than he cares for. He might just as well bleat to the sheep in the field for all the sympathy he's going to get. All that keepers interested in is how he's going to pay his bill. The rest is water off a duck's back. And as for myself, I gave such a lame description that it could be anyone, so you have no worries there. You're both as safe as the king in his castle.'

Jerry chortled. 'Good, good, that's pleasing to my ears. Now how do you feel about us helping you with a nice little earner from today's takings?' Jerry pushed a purse towards Richard, containing the equivalent of a fortnight's wages. The highwaymen talked Richard's language. He smiled broadly at the two men.

'What's your name?' asked Jerry.

'Richard. Richard Ferguson,' came the reply.

'Well, Dick Ferguson, it might be of some interest to you, if you fancy upping your earnings in this world, to have supper with us this evening. After all, Nancy doesn't come cheap and your wages can't possibly sustain the lifestyle you're obviously seeking,' said Jerry, his eyes looking coyly at those of Richard, making him blush with embarrassment.

Richard's game was up, and his pretence as gentry had been blown out of the water. He just hoped the outlaws wouldn't say a word to Nancy. He turned his half-cupped hand and looked at the purse resting within.

'If this is a sign of things to come, you have my interest,' said Richard.

Jerry nodded. 'Meet us at the Bald Faced Stag, Putney Vale. Eight-thirty, sharp.'

With his new-found supply of cash, the young postilion raced back home. The wind had begun to ease slightly, and things seemed a little calmer, in more ways than one.

Without a second thought, he took it upon himself to go over to Nancy's earlier than planned, in order to keep his promise to meet with Jerry and Henry later that evening.

After repeatedly knocking her door, it was eventually opened sharply.

'Why are you so early? You can't come in, I'm otherwise engaged. Return at your scheduled time,' came Nancy's icy greeting as the door was disrespectfully slammed in Richard's face.

The harsh reality of being taken for a dupe hit home hard. The realisation of being thought no better than the last stranger to leave her room cut Richard to the bone. Enraged by the dismissive reception bestowed upon him, he stormed from the house, vowing it to be the last time he would be made a fool of by a woman.

Still licking his wounds, Richard set about making his way back to his lodgings, whereupon, by pure chance, he crossed the path of Henry Watts.

'Twice in one day,' quipped Henry.

'Three, if you're counting,' retorted Richard.

Henry cocked his head back and laughed. 'Suppose it is if you look at it that way. Are you still up for this evening?'

'Hell, yes. Are you heading over there now?' asked Richard, his thoughts of Nancy mellowing somewhat. 'I am Dick Ferguson, that I am.'

'Good, then I'll come with you.'

Apprehension is rarely without good cause, and as the two men neared the Bald Faced Stag, Richard grew increasingly aware of the environment he was about to enter. A carefree stroll into church on a crisp Sunday morning, followed by a light-hearted chat with the reverend over the meaning of life didn't ring any bells of comparability.

As Richard trotted his horse past the inn's imposing frontage, it was clear for all to see that the old building held sway as a landmark of profound coaching history, standing with dominance beside the long straight road that led to the dusty, smoke-riddled metropolis neighbouring old Father Thames.

A single white column stood either side of the inn's large, heavy, black-panelled door, like guards of the realm forever on duty. Richard grinned to himself as he viewed its external grandeur, dressed extensively in a dark green coat of creeping ivy, which totally belied the villainy that lay within its walls.

All feelings of uncertainty were soon proved unfounded when the outlaws received him with every mark of endearment. The men all shared the same, sometimes dark, sometimes crude humour, which was, with good reason, frowned upon at his place of employment, where suppression of such talk was key to keeping one's weekly wages intact.

Richard sat quietly, listening, smiling and laughing at the never-ending onslaught of humorous tales recalled from their previous day's exploits; not so much that he was timid or shy, but because he was instinctively using his sense of observation, which had been instilled into him as a child by his mother on their regular Sunday afternoon walks in the Hereford countryside.

His observations weren't without results, as he witnessed an intriguing phenomenon unravel before his eyes. This large group of men were without the usual irritable rodent that so often reared its ugly head as he shuttled his passengers to and forth during his busy day. *There must be one in here surely? There's always at least one cow pat in every field*, he told himself, but here he found it not to be the case. These men were very, very close indeed, and very, very comfortable in one another's company.

The evening was passing quickly. Three hours seemed like one, which is quite the usual when you're enjoying good company. The ale was still flowing fast and furiously, although all the food had long since been devoured. Richard found himself making particularly good acquaintance with a straight-talking young man who didn't mince his words and always seemed to have an answer. Even when it was blatantly obvious that he was wrong, he would continue the argument until the cows came home, waiting for you to explain yourself away and prove your point and drive that final nail into his coffin with "I told you so glee". At this point, he would break into a broad "gotcha" smile, making your hard-earned victory seem hollow, diminished and just a tad embarrassing, as all who gathered around laughed hysterically, knowing you'd been sucked in and spat out by a master of tongue-in-cheek horseplay.

The man's name was Billy Frampton, the nephew of Jumping Joe, the close childhood friend of Jerry and Henry, who only a short time earlier had met his long-awaited appointment with the hangman, having been captured and brought to justice after a failed robbery on the king's highway.

Richard and Billy instantly took to one another, their humour bouncing back and forth, picking up pace as each minute passed. There was no refrain from either man as they watched with amusement as Jerry drunkenly lurched towards them from across the crowded room and planted himself down with a thud beside them, whilst ignoring their intoxicated boyish chuckles.

'Well, Dick Ferguson, have you thought any further about becoming one of our number?' slurred Jerry, with his eyes more in control than he let on. Richard brandished an ear to ear smile and raised his half-filled tankard.

Billy Frampton glanced at Jerry. 'I think that smile says more than a thousand words ever could,' he said.

Jerry closed his eyes, smiled and nodded before climbing to his feet. 'We'll talk again in the morning, Dick Ferguson. There's much to discuss.'

******

In the Bald Faced Stag the following morning, Jerry was busy telling Richard what he had in mind for him. 'We think you're in a prime position to help us gather information on the comings and goings of the more affluent in our society. Lodging where you are, above the coach house in Piccadilly, gives you great opportunity and scope to chat with the coachmen, ostlers and the like and glean as much information as possible about the times they set off on their journeys, their destinations and, more importantly, the social standing of the passengers.

'The more you find out about who we would be dealing with, the better it is for all of us. It will also be very beneficial to you, Dick. And here's the best part; you'll not be at any risk of getting your collar felt. It will be us who are risking our necks. Be discreet and don't be pushy, you don't want to raise any suspicion. For your good work you'll receive an equal cut of the spoils. If you encounter any problems with over-inquisitive types, let us know immediately, and they'll be dealt with. Remember, you're one of us now.'

It wasn't long before Dick was sharing inconceivable sums of illicit money, way beyond his wildest imaginings, which he, without remorse, frittered freely away. The party lasted for just over a year, until his heavy consumption of wine, women and song rendered him incapable of fulfilling his duties to his employer, leading to yet another undignified dismissal from his place of employment.

The Bald-Faced Stag Inn, Putney Vale
5 May 1795, 9 am

HENRY WAS sitting alone, enjoying breakfast. It was his everyday favourite, four rashers of thick-cut bacon, two eggs, served with fresh bread, and a cup of piping hot coffee. He was more than content to be left in peace to devour his food without interruption before setting about his day. Unfortunately, that small but significant moment of paradise wasn't to be. His peace of mind was broken upon the arrival of Dick Ferguson. Henry groaned to himself in despair, knowing it wasn't going to be good news with such an early arrival. Dick wasn't one of life's early risers without good reason.

'Morning, Henry,' Dick whispered sheepishly. 'Morning. Go get yourself a coffee and breakfast, and put it on my bill,' said Henry, still deeply engrossed in his early morning feast.

Dick ordered his food and joined his friend at his table, hesitating slightly before plucking up the courage to spit out the words that had nervously stuck to the back of his throat. 'I've just been dismissed from my job. They told me I was unreliable.'

Henry looked neither shocked nor surprised at the disclosure of the bad news. 'They weren't wrong, were they?' came his unsympathetic reply. Jerry and Henry had watched Dick's ill-fated journey towards unemployment unravel slowly before them for some time. The writing had been well and truly on the wall, and it was just a matter of when. Henry was surprised it had lasted as long as it did.

The familiar echo of Jerry's sure-footed steps trudging down the staircase took their attention.

'What's going on?' Jerry asked, as he lazily scratched his head, yawning.

'Dick has been booted out of his job,' remarked Henry matter-of-factly. Jerry called to the landlord for some coffee and boiled eggs.

'Nothing lasts forever,' Jerry remarked half-heartedly to his friends. Dick looked bemused, believing they would be angry with his disclosure, but things were unfolding far more favourably than he'd expected.

Feeling relieved, Dick decided to approach his friends in the same uncaring manner. 'It looks like I'm going to have to take to the highway to earn a crust,' he murmured tentatively, as he stared into his coffee.

'Looks that way because I'm not buying you breakfast every bloody morning,' said Henry, as he washed down the last of his meal with his coffee.

******

Winterman's brandy shop sat in a narrow, dingy, although bustling street, within a stone's throw of St Paul's Cathedral. Nesting unceremoniously between two larger, more dominant buildings, it was devoid of the slightest hint of sunlight. Its proprietor was a man much marked with smallpox. Short in stature, with a protruding beer belly and high-pitched voice, he was a cocky but also cowardly man, brought up under the protection of his older, bigger brothers, which gave him the obvious confidence to continue his crude and irritating ways through to adulthood. He was thirty-nine years of age, but you could be forgiven in believing him to be of more advanced years.

This was "Wolf" Winterman. His family were all scavengers and smugglers who lived in and out of each other's pockets from day to day. He'd lost his mother to smallpox when he was only seven and was then transferred from the protective wing of his mother to the drunken hands of his gin-soaked father. He soon grew up to be a smuggler himself, developing a very cunning and astute business brain, way beyond that of his elders, which was deceptive to say the least, considering his outward appearance and crass, vulgar mannerisms.

If he'd channelled his criminal enthusiasm into the right direction, it would undoubtedly have served him well in life but, alas, the man was what he was and his adrenalin-fuelled kicks came from the anticipation of the next stolen item that made its way to his highly polished shop counter, giving him grotesquely indecent profit margins without the effort of venturing too far from his shop doorway.

The company that inhabited his residence were the less decent of society, ranging from footpads and whores to the hierarchy of the criminal underworld, the highwaymen. Each and every one knew they could unload their properties from their audacious deeds via Wolf. Jerry Avershaw and Henry Watts were no exception, and they routinely fenced a large majority of their booty through Wolf, sometimes visiting his brandy shop, but more often than not meeting with him at the Oxford Arms, a short walk around the corner in Warwick Lane, where they felt safer and more at ease.

Wolf would be found here on a regular basis, drinking with his brothers and one or two of their lowly sidekicks. Even drinking here had its calculated reasons for Wolf, as all of the stagecoaches departed from here for Chester, Highworth in Wiltshire and Wendover in Buckinghamshire.

He paid his informers for "quality information", as he would put it, and then pass it on to Jerry and Henry for a share of the spoils. The high tobys were in awe of Wolf's long and ongoing achievements – after all, they had tried it themselves through Dick and it had only lasted fourteen months.

The robberies linked to the Oxford Arms were limited to only every so often, for specially selected, excruciatingly wealthy travellers, so as not to arouse the slightest of suspicion. This was Wolf's manor and nobody else could work this inn without dire consequences ensuing. He had total control, the system had worked well for several years and he knew what he was doing.

On this particular day, Jerry and Henry had good reason to meet with Wolf at his shop, as they were going to introduce him to a new partner of theirs, someone who would be partaking in regular "business transactions" with him – Dick Ferguson.

'Come in. Come in. Good to see ya, Jerry. Henry, Henry… how are ya, me old son?' said Wolf Winterman in his excited, high-pitched voice. 'And who do we 'ave 'ere then. A new fresh face, that's for sure.' Wolf's devious, calculating eyes looked Dick up and down from head to toe, while smiling a crocodile smile.

'We would like you to meet our new business partner. He's been in our company for over a year now. This is Dick Ferguson. You'll be seeing a lot more of him in the near future, and all for the benefit of everyone we hope,' said Jerry in a friendly but no-nonsense tone, reminding their cunning fence that no liberties would be tolerated with their friend.

'Treat me fair, I treat you fair. That's how it works,' said Wolf. 'Nice to meet with your acquaintance, Dick.'

'The feeling's mutual Wolf,' replied Dick. 'I'm looking forward to doing business with you.'

Dick smiled as he looked over Wolf's counter at a gold-framed sign that was hanging on a finely decorated wall for all visitors to see. It read:

Beware and take care
When things they look fair
For in life you will find
They are not.

Wolf Winterman had obviously been bitten in the past by another dog far more insidiously cunning than himself and had learned his lesson the hard way. *That sign isn't given pride of place in his shop for the benefit of his lowly customers*, Dick thought to himself. *That sign's up there in all its glory to remind himself on a daily basis.*

'Let me tell you an interesting little story, Dicky my old son,' said Wolf. 'I'm sure the lads won't mind.' Jerry and Henry groaned and turned away in disbelief, knowing what was coming. They had heard it all before.

Wolf poured them each a large brandy from his smuggled stock, to hold their attention during his tale. 'My brother Aldus took a trip to Wiltshire on a bit of business. On his arrival he was panting like a dog on a hot summer day, so he made his way to the bar and sat himself down to enjoy an ale or two. He was drawn into a conversation with a couple of young scallywags who turned out to be local high tobys. Well, the more ale that was done, the looser the tongue, and they began to tell him a sob story of their frustrations on the road. Apparently, on more than one occasion they lay in wait to rob the London to Highworth coach, only to find that it had already been turned over by highwaymen on the outskirts of London.'

Wolf started to giggle like a little boy. 'I wonder who that could have been,' he added.

Dick smiled at his story. 'Really?' he remarked.

Wolf nodded in the direction of Dick's friends. 'Yeah, really. And most of the spoils came to me. Small world, innit.'

The Sword Blade Coffee House,
Birching Lane, 8 May 1795, 10 am

' A MAIN of cocks are to be fought at Herbert Brown's new pit, at the sign of the Black Bull later this morning. Do you fancy going over and having a flutter?' Jerry asked Dick as they neared the Sword Blade Coffee House.

'Why not?' said Dick. 'If we don't, it's going to be one of those long-drawn-out days, I can see it coming. But let's stop here and have a coffee first.'

As they drank their coffee, Dick asked Jerry, 'How did life come to deal you the hand you have?' Dick flicked at the top of his coffee, as if something undesirable had just plonked itself into it.

'Well, if the truth be known, we can't all be Admiral Hood now, can we?' Jerry replied. 'As much as any young boy dreamed of being such a hero, if someone like me joined our Navy, they would have to start right down there at the bottom of the pile, alongside the pressed and the likes. Then after many a year of sailing the sea, and if I'm still alive and kicking, guess where I would be...you guessed it, right there in the same place, at the bottom of that bloody pile.

'So, I decided to follow my natural progression because, quite simply, I didn't fancy working in a factory or mopping the decks. As I see it, it's all about circumstances – where you're born, and of course to whom. That's what dictates whether you have half a chance in this world. You also have to take into account that whatever environment you live in has some type of role model to which you can aspire. You know what I mean, that someone who jumps out at you at that decisive point in your life and gives you inspiration and that little bit of extra motivation to be the same as them. And where I came from, we were pretty short on admirals and judges. But the high toby...now there's a different story.

'Working in factories from dawn to dusk, seven days a week, crippling the only body life gave you, not to mention your heart and soul, isn't in my mind the way to go about things. I'd sooner take my chances in the other direction, and so far, so good. And as you found out that evening you were invited over to meet my friends for the first time, you couldn't help but notice that I wasn't alone in thinking along these lines. The girls from our manor were no different. The factories were their only option too, or maybe a domestic, so many drifted into the world of whoring, and the prettier ones became courtesans.'

Jerry pondered over his thoughts for a second or two before breaking out into a short, sharp smile and continuing. 'I suppose if the roles of the sexes were to be reversed, and I was to expect women to pay for my favours, I'd have starved to death a long time ago. Unless I could find myself a nice handful of wealthy lonely spinsters in dire need of some company. That just might keep my head above the water. Do you see where I'm coming from, Dick?

Look, what I'm trying to say is these boys of ours like to take one path, and the girls do the same, but in a different way. You use the tools you were given. The likes of me will always be no different, and the likes of Nancy will always be Nancys. That's what I'm trying to say.'

'Do you still venture over to Nancy's, Jerry?' Dick asked sombrely, hoping for an answer that pleased. Jerry glared in bewilderment. Obviously, Dick's feelings for her still ran high, and Jerry was trying his damnedest to understand how anyone could be drawn in by such a woman.

Subtlety was not the strongest link in Jerry's armour, although he tried his utmost to dissolve any lingering emotions his friend held for Nancy. 'Sometimes, Dick, you meet with a pretty woman, with an engaging smile and a twinkle in her eye. In fact, she's so darned fetching, you just can't take your eyes off her. She looks back at you and see's you staring at her, all googly eyed and looking stupid, and she'll do one of three things. She may dismiss you completely, as she's not interested for one reason or another. She may have taken a shine to you, the same way you did her. Or she may be like Nancy, who uses her charms to gain money and gifts.

'The Nancy's of this world can't afford to fall in love. They're on the treadmill, and don't need the hassle of a jealous boyfriend. You have to understand their reasoning. For most of the girls, their lives will be permanent doom and gloom to the bitter end, although some of the shrewder courtesans are wise enough to tuck away much of their earnings to safeguard their futures.

They're aware of the short shelf life their profession entails, and they usually want to duck out of it at the first God-given opportunity, so you can see why they're so hard-nosed. How can you blame them?

'When that time comes – when they feel financially secure – then and only then they just might set about looking for agent with a purse substantially bigger than their own to settle down with, but that isn't something to be taken for granted. The toffs love their fun and games with them, but that's usually where it ends. Settling down with such a woman usually doesn't enter their line of thought, although there are sometimes exceptions. So, you see, they set out in life with a dilemma and end their working days with yet another dilemma. Do you see a pattern forming, Dick?'

Jerry allowed himself a titter, adding, 'I remember Nancy once told me that the only thing people give you for nothing is grief. Everything else comes at a price. I often wonder at those words, and to tell you the truth, with the exception of close friends and family, I think she hit the nail bang on the head.

'And while I'm on a roll, I'll tell you another thing. No matter how hard you try to steer these women back on course, it won't happen. You might just as well take yourself down to the knacker's yard and set about flogging a dead horse until you're red in the face with exhaustion. But for all I say, I don't look down on the Nancys of this world, that's why I'm sorry if it hurts you, Dick, but I still make my visits. For I'm no better and don't need the complications either.'

******

That same afternoon, an elegantly dressed woman made her way through the gateway of the Vauxhall Pleasure Gardens, with an air of sophisticated composure likened to that of a princess. Her glistening auburn hair cascaded meticulously between her slender shoulder blades in flowing curls.

Jerry and Henry observed her with interest as she sailed by, making her way towards the sound of singing violins. She was accompanied by a sharply dressed man with mannerisms that bordered on the effeminate, giving the impression of one that had a cosy, sheltered existence. They paused momentarily before placing themselves down in their seats to enjoy the music of the orchestra.

'Where have I seen that woman before?' asked Henry with a hint of embarrassment, wondering to himself how he could misplace such an attractive woman.

Jerry gave an agreeable nod whilst still watching intently. 'Funny you should say that. I was thinking the self-same thing. Our paths have crossed at some point in the past, but where and when, I can't be sure.'

As Jerry lay in his bed that evening, he found himself restless, struggling to get to sleep. His mind was racing, and he became frustrated with the arduous task of trying to recollect where he'd seen the mystery woman who had visited the Pleasure Gardens earlier that evening.

He thought and thought, but his efforts were to no avail, eventually succumbing to the inevitable, and drifting into slumber, only to be awakened moments later by a knock on the door. It was Henry, who had been thinking about the same encounter, but with far greater success.

'Jerry, Jerry. The woman at the Pleasure Gardens earlier,' Henry said excitedly. 'I remember her. She was Charles Stokes' fiancée and attended the assizes with the Stokes family. She wore a hat, had her hair tied back and wore a shawl draped over her shoulders, which she used to cover much of her face. She always placed herself as far back as possible from them, but that was her for sure. Do you want to see her again?'

'More than words can say, Henry,' replied Jerry. 'I haven't satisfied myself with that family. Our Jenny may have, but that little privilege is yet to come my way. It would be very comforting to separate her from everything she possesses, don't you think?'

Henry smiled, replying, 'Well, these people buy themselves homes all over London, just for easy access to the theatres and Pleasure Gardens, so I'd bet my horse that she returns there on a regular basis.'

******

The vibrant atmosphere of the gardens made for the perfect environment to mingle indiscriminately, and James Myers and Dick Ferguson exploited it to its full, as they casually wandered arm in arm with their paid company.

Meanwhile, Jerry and Henry took on a far more static but just as important role, placing themselves within view of the garden's giant, heavily scrolled, wrought iron gates, in the hope of catching sight of the woman they so desperately wanted to wreak revenge upon. They stood smoking, talking and watching, and then watching some more.

Henry's alert eyes picked up on two figures weaving their way through the crowd with urgency. It was James, followed closely by his escort. He looked agitated and concerned as he approached Jerry and Henry.

'Mathew Caplin is here,' James told them. 'I've just seen him. He's alone. I watched him for a few minutes or so, and I get the impression he's waiting for someone.'

'Are you sure it's him?' asked Henry inquisitively. 'Oh, yes. No doubt about it. It's him alright. Come and take a look for yourselves.' Jerry and Henry didn't need to be asked twice.

As they followed their guides closely through the crowd, James turned abruptly towards his friends and pointed sneakily, saying, 'He's some way over there. Stay here while me and my lady get closer. We'll walk within a cart's length before turning sharply away.' Jerry removed his spyglass and focused it on his moving friend as he followed through on his promise, giving him a clear view.

'Well, well, well. What have we here then?' said Jerry. Henry stared at his friend, the frustration in his eyes clear to see, wishing he'd carried such a handy instrument in his own pocket.

'What do you see? Come on, tell me,' Henry asked eagerly.

'Our little bit of posh is talking to Mathew Caplin. The cheeky little monkey must have slipped in through a different gate. Crafty, crafty, crafty.' Jerry retracted his spyglass and placed it back into his pocket. 'I would say our little lady isn't to be underestimated and I would wager this cosy little meeting has much to do about us.'

Henry absorbed his friend's words, before moving closer to witness the pair talking. 'She isn't going to let this matter rest until she sees our rotting corpses hanging high,' said Henry. 'Now we know why she was so shy at the assizes. She's out for revenge, and this is why she's having this meeting with the bastard.'

The two highwaymen returned to the gate, awaiting the arrival of their friends. The moment they arrived, James was pulled to one side, out of earshot of the courtesans.

'You must watch the posh one incessantly,' Jerry told him. 'As soon as she takes her leave, you must dismiss Dick and the girls and follow her to her place of residence. You must work alone. Meet with us afterwards at the Bald Faced Stag. Don't fail me now!'

Later, James Myers marched military fashion into the Bald Faced Stag, closing the door sharply behind him.

'Any success?' asked Jerry, his mood calm and collected, although hoping his short and to the point question didn't indicate a profound lack of confidence in his friend's achievements.

'Yeah. I followed lady posh to her residence, Castle Street, Leicester Square. That's where she lives. She was chaperoned home by the bastard. That man is one cunning, devious pit dog. When they stopped their carriage and she stepped out, he took her hand and kissed it like a proper gent, before sending her on her way down the road and around the corner by foot. That was the awkward part for me because I had to leave my carriage and follow her, and he was still hanging around watching until she turned the corner out of view, before telling his coachman to leave. I then had to run like the wind down the road and into Castle Street to see where she was.

Fortunately for me she lived a fair way down, so it gave me time to see her enter. I think there's more than a bit of business going on between them. He looked too interested in her, but we'll have to watch like hawks and see what unfolds.'

Jerry thought for a while before commenting, 'The fact that she stepped from the carriage early and made the rest of her journey on foot justifies my thoughts on why they arranged to meet at the Pleasure Gardens and not at her home or Caplin's office. They wanted to keep their little rendezvous discreet. They don't want anybody to know what they're up to.'

Henry interrupted. 'Look, we all know Caplin's aware that it was us that robbed the home of Stokes, with George, Ned and Thomas. And if he knows, she knows. Simple as that. But one thing's for sure, they can't prove a thing. If the Runners aren't coming for us, why should Caplin be any different? They know they have to find a lot more than they have to offer, and it simply isn't there for them. She's clearly seeking satisfaction and I dare say the same goes for Caplin to a degree, but as far as I can see, they only have one option open to them, and that's to set us up.'

A loud murmur of assent from the other three outlaws filled the room, as they absorbed Henry's words.

'James,' said Jerry, 'take Billy with you first thing tomorrow morning and run an eye over her house. Let's see what can be unearthed. Try to find any weak links amongst the staff, especially the domestics. They're the ones who get kicked about the most. You know what to look for. Po-faced, fed up disgruntled looks, that kind of thing. They all have to leave the house at some point in time, and when they do it's up to you to pick and choose who's worth striking up a conversation with. If you feel you have half a chance, go to work on them, but remember, if they look unapproachable, it's because they are.'

The Sword Blade Coffee House, Birching Lane

10 May 1795, 1.45 pm

JERRY SAT in the corner of the room facing the door, drawing short, speedy sips from his coffee cup, before placing it back down on the table in the same brisk fashion. Henry and Dick watched their agitated friend with wry smiles. 'Where are James and Billy? They were supposed to be here at half past one,' said Jerry. Henry chortled under his breath, amused at his friend's scathing remark.

'What's so funny?' asked Dick, bemused at Henry's prolonged amusement.

'Jerry made a present of an Eardley Norton quarter repeater silver pocket watch to James for his birthday,' Henry explained. 'I'd have liked it for myself, I tell you. It's a beauty. But since James has had it, his timekeeping hasn't changed none. He's still always late.'

Jerry straightened in his chair, ignoring his friend's words. 'Well, talk of the devil. Look who's here,' he said. James glanced at Jerry sheepishly, deciding to ignore the path of lame excuses that might inflame things further.

'Sorry, we're a bit late, Jerry.'

'Not as sorry as I am,' replied Jerry. 'I give you a handsome timepiece for your birthday, and you may as well leave it in your bedside drawer. I've never seen you make good use of it. And why are the two of you looking so pleased with yourselves, wearing those ridiculous smiles?'

'We were only outside the lady's house fifteen minutes when a skivvy came trudging out on an errand, looking sadder than a pig in a butcher's shop. Billy approached her and struck up a conversation. It turned out she's only been employed there two and a half months. Worked her fingers to the bone she has, only to be told by the houseboy that things weren't looking good there. Apparently, he'd overheard the butler talking to the housemaid about the house being in grave financial difficulties, and it probably wouldn't be long before they would all be regrettably dismissed. Isn't that right Billy?'

'Aye,' Billy replied. 'I told her I'll return tomorrow at midday and will pay her handsomely for any further information she's able to glean. I also told her that she mustn't tell a soul, as much as she might be tempted. She told me to rest my nerves, as it wouldn't be in her best interests to tell anyone, as it could result in negative consequences for her future employment. But she'll try to find out because she could do with the money.'

'Let's try to climb inside their minds,' said Henry. 'Lady posh and Caplin are pretty much certain we're who they're looking for when it comes to the robbery of Stokes's home, and the cutting down of George, Ned and Thomas must also rankle heavily. Caplin has failed miserably in bringing us to justice, and that of course is damaging to his ego, never mind his reputation. Lady posh, on the other hand, must lie in her bed, night after night, pondering over who it was who took the lives of her future husband and father-in-law, itching to bite back like an angry viper. We can be sure their book of revenge won't be closed until we're dealt with.'

The Bald-Faced Stag Inn, Putney Vale
14 May 1795, 12.50 pm

'WELL, BILLY, did your new-found best friend tell you anything that might be of significance to us?' asked Henry with spiked interest.

'Aye. She was waiting for me at twelve o'clock sharp,' replied Billy.

Jerry interrupted. 'Did you hear that, Henry? He must have sold her that watch I gave James for his birthday?'

Billy gave a rueful smile before continuing. 'To be honest, I felt sorry for her. She's a pretty girl, with the rarity of unblemished skin, but when you look at her hands, they're a different story. Dry, cracked and weeping they are. They look more like the hands of a navvy. She told me of an interesting occurrence that took place this morning though. Two strange men were methodically sifting through the house, room by room. She'd been told to give them a wide berth because they were busy assessing the property for improvements. She didn't fall for that one though, not after hearing of the financial difficulties.

'She also didn't believe the men were workmen. She said they were too cocksure and carried a military-like assertiveness about them. She also noticed many of the valuables had been picked up and replaced skew-whiff, much to her annoyance, for it was her who cleaned and dusted them every day before placing them back in their places with precise, meticulous care. The houseboy didn't have any further information to give her unfortunately. Oh, and by the way, we have her name. She's called Catherine Jane Forster.'

******

That evening, Jerry and Henry were riding through the fog. 'We're being followed,' groaned Jerry, as he trotted his horse beside that of Henry.

'I know. They've been tailing us for five minutes or so,' replied Henry, without the slightest hint of a turned head. 'Maybe we should retreat to the Green Man instead. There should be a fair number in there this evening, and it might be enough to discourage our followers.'

Jerry cracked an uncaring grimace, his eyes still engrossed with the murky road in front of him. 'I think so, my friend. The Green Man it is.'

A short time later, the two were ensconced in the Green Man. 'I wonder whether the two wretches that followed us earlier were the same pair who were giving Catherine Forster's home the once over,' mused Jerry. 'Things are beginning to piece together. Forster with Caplin at the Pleasure Gardens. The monitoring of our whereabouts. It's all for good reason, and I think the reason is that they're planning to remove all items of value from the house. Why else would they have checked everything over so thoroughly?' Jerry continued. 'Once they've done this, they'll call in the Bow Street Runners, claiming a robbery has taken place. Of course, during the night, making the crime more serious, due to the fact the thieves were in the property while its occupants were all sound asleep. The Runners will of course take note of the crime but will have no evidence to follow up on an arrest. This, our friend Caplin will be fully aware of.

'Catherine Forster will then hire the services of Caplin, in the hope of retrieving her stolen goods and bringing those responsible to justice. I dare say Caplin will then revert back to his old familiar ways and use fabricated witnesses, as he's done so often in the past, to give statements claiming they saw us leaving the property in the early hours. And, of course, let's not overlook the devious but predictable planting of some of the stolen items upon our person to seal our fate.'

'It sounds feasible, Jerry,' agreed Henry. 'I just hope we're not overthinking things, but if what you say is correct and Caplin and Forster are plotting to bring us down with the claim of us robbing her home, I can't help but think we have a war on our hands. After all, we were going to do just that to her – rob her home for revenge – and if we did, we'd have been playing right into their hands. Would you bloody believe it?'

'Billy, James,' Jerry announced. 'You must stay in contact with the house girl. We're one step ahead of them at the moment, as they're unaware of all we know, and this may give us a window of opportunity to turn the tables on them. The girl is going through a worrying and stressful time at the moment, and this may just be the key to obliterating Caplin and Forster. If our girl is strong in mind and prepared to go the extra mile for a capital sum of money, we may well have found our solution. You two must return to her immediately and offer her a proposition she can't refuse.'

The George Inn, Southwark
15 May 1795, 2 pm

'DID YOU make sure you weren't followed?' asked a concerned Henry.

'Don't worry yourself, Henry. We made our way over on foot, using the alleys and courtyards,' replied Billy reassuringly.

'Well, what did she have to say?' asked Henry.

'She grabbed at the offer with desperation in her eyes.' Billy's indignant words mellowed to no more than a tremor. 'That girl doesn't deserve the hand she's been dealt in life, I can tell you.'

Billy's warming to the girl made for simmering anger among the tetchy outlaws, who viewed his emotional signs of caring and protectiveness as frailty, open to exploitation. 'Go stand in front of a bloody mirror and look hard at yourself!' barked Henry. 'What you see in front of you is the same thing. Stop feeling sorry for someone who's no different to yourself. Just focus on your priorities, Billy, and eradicate all personal feeling from that soft sentimental head of yours. We have this girl eating from our hand, and she may well be the ace in the pack that will save us from a cart ride to the gallows. So, don't leave yourself open to anything that may lead to us falling out.' Henry stared with ice-cold belligerence. His message was not shrouded in subtleties.

'You have no worries here, Henry. You can rest assured of that,' replied Billy, concealing his nervous disposition with grand accomplishment.

'Good, good,' replied Henry. 'Now let's start again, but without the nonsense.'

Billy continued his tale. 'She was in a state of absolute misery when we caught up with her. She knows the clock's ticking and it won't be long before she's out on her ear without a roof over her head. I think she needs us as much as we need her. She asked why we were so intent on meddling into Forster's comings and goings, so we told her we were two disgruntled ex-staff who had been unfairly dismissed on unfounded hearsay. Sometimes unwarranted mud sticks and, in our case, it's done just that. So, all we wish to do is return the favour. There's nothing wrong with that, is there?

'She seemed satisfied with our cock and bull story, although personally I don't think she really cared. Her thoughts seemed to be elsewhere. I then told her we'd discovered who the two strange men in the house were, and that they were part of a scam to remove the valuables from within to make it look like a brazen robbery had taken place, so the valuables weren't being taken and used to recuperate Forster's outstanding debts. Also, Forster would claim off her insurance policy for a pretty sum.

'I told the girl that we also didn't think it would end there, and there was every possibility that Forster's possessions would then be sold on for further prosperity and financial peace of mind. The day these items walk out of that house, will be the day her employment will be terminated. We also told her, word for word, everything you told us to say.'

'Good, good,' replied Jerry. 'Go see her tomorrow. She must have a word with John Townsend.'

Leicester Square, London
16 May 1795, 12 Noon

'GO TO Union Hall, Southwark, and ask for John Townsend,' Billy instructed the girl. 'Speak to him and him only, do you understand me?' The girl nodded with focused attention, acknowledging Billy's words with all seriousness.

Billy continued his instructions. 'You must tell him of what you believe is taking place at the house, and of course you must inform him that a man by the name of Mathew Caplin is behind the scam. You know of this because you overheard the men in the house talking of him. This should spike his interest. He's a very, very astute old fox, with a wealth of worldly knowledge behind him, and we're aware that he neither likes nor trusts Caplin.

'He's fully aware of the countless unlawful acts that Caplin has participated in over the years in order to gain his convictions, and he's also aware that Caplin has lined his pockets heartily from the proceeds. He'll not let such an opportunity to bring him to justice pass him by. You don't take a fox to a chicken run and expect it to turn its back on it, do you?

'If Townsend asks why you asked specifically to speak to him, tell him you were far too scared to talk to anyone else, for fear of it getting back to these people. And then butter him up a bit by telling him you know you can trust him, as he's a pillar of society and a good friend of our godly king. This will undoubtedly lift his spirits and place you firmly in his corner.'

******

Later that evening, Billy and James met up with the girl again. 'Did you manage to make contact with him?' Billy asked.

'Yes, Billy. I spoke to him and made him aware of everything, word for word, line by line. I knew I only had one bite at the apple, so I had to make sure I didn't ruin the opportunity. Mr Townsend listened intently to what I had to say. He's such a nice man. He put me at my ease straight away by asking my name. When I told him, it was Rosie Hopkins and that I came from Shoreditch, he smiled and said, "Well, enlighten me with what you have to say, Rosie from Shoreditch."'

'You were right,' Rosie continued, 'he's a very worldly man and quite a character. I found him to be very light-hearted with me, but I did, for a fleeting moment, catch another side to his personality when we were interrupted during our conversation by one of his officers, and his mannerism and posture took on a completely different mantle. That was when I knew I was dealing with someone who has a very different perspective on life when crossed.

'He asked me if my room was close to any of the rooms that had been visited by the two sinister men. I told him that it was. He then told me to return to my address and watch and listen for anything untoward taking place, and if I see anything, to make a note of it and at once deliver it to a man who can be found at the end of my road sitting on a bench, with a book or newspaper and a bag by his side with the initials JT emblazoned upon it.

'He then went on to tell me that the initials on the man's bag are the same as his because the bag belongs to him, so I would know I was approaching the correct person. And if the weather decides to take a turn for the worse, my man will be found in Sharps coffee house next door. I only have to pop my head inside the door, and he'll come to me, of course carrying Mr Townsend's wonderful initialled bag that he said had cost him far more than he should have squandered.'

Rosie chuckled, then carried on. 'I told you he was funny. He then told me to carry on as normal and not to concern myself with any of the events that may take place after nightfall. He was very adamant about that. He told me he didn't want me to put myself at risk of anything nasty. That was all he had to say to me. He then kindly made me a cup of tea and mentioned that if a conviction materialises from my information, he'll personally make it his business to see that I'm rewarded for being a good citizen of the community. He then sent me on my way. It seems to me your revenge now lies in his hands.'

Billy and James looked at one another despondently. They weren't the words they wanted to hear. They were hoping for a clear description of the Runner's plan of action, but John Townsend was, as always, keeping his cards very close to his chest.

Slaughters Coffee House, St Martins Lane, London 20 May 1795, 10 am

THERE WAS a comfortable silence between Jerry and Henry as they sat with their coffee, absorbing the comings and goings of the many locals who frequented the always busy coffee house. The two outlaws eventually rested their eyes upon a nearby table, which seated three well-heeled young men of much the same age as themselves.

However, age was as much as the two parties shared in common, as it was clear for all to see that the hardship and misery encountered by those less fortunate had not at any time of the three young men's lives met with their acquaintance. They were whinging consistently about the miserable consequences that their god-forsaken riches had bestowed upon them.

Henry, upon hearing their indecently embarrassing chants, quipped under a breath of cynicism, 'Lend me your hat, Jerry. I'm going to have a quick whip-around for the poor bastards.'

His words fell on deaf ears. Henry watched his friend's fixation with one of the men, whose flamboyant, exaggerated mannerisms were of great amusement to him. Henry became conscious of his friend's mood. The signs of his up-and-down personality were about to rise to the surface, and it was only a matter of time before they came into view.

Jerry didn't have to wait long for his opportunity to unleash his timely interruption into the men's conversation, for they were forever quoting poems and idioms from the likes of William Shakespeare. Their conversation then took a turn on to the London party scene, with which they were all so familiar.

The genteel gent climbed from his chair before dramatically waving his arms in the air in the manner of a promising young thespian, and made yet another quote, this one from Samuel Johnson: 'Sir, when a man is tired of London, he is tired of life, for there is in London all that life can afford.'

Jerry saw his moment to interject. 'Said the man from inherited wealth who could afford it.' The three men turned to see who dared interrupt their cosy conversation with such an inflammatory remark, only to be confronted with ice-cold stares from the aggressive highwaymen. The three men turned away to avoid the situation proceeding to the next level and took their leave.

'See, Henry,' exclaimed Jerry, 'where can you find yourself this kind of fun in Southwark?'

Henry took a sip of his coffee before replying, 'I know. It's one extreme to another. Halfwits or jesters…take your choice. Maybe one day we'll find a place somewhere in the middle to sip our coffee.'

Jerry smiled. 'Naw. Somewhere in the middle doesn't exist,' he said.

The Bald-Faced Stag Inn, Putney Vale
21 May 1795, 1 pm

BILLY AND James dismounted from their steaming, exhausted horses, bestowing their trusted steeds into the care of old Ralph, before hastily making their way into the shelter of the inn, where Jerry, Dick and Henry were perched by the fireside.

'Rosie has just informed us that the house was cleared in the early hours of this morning,' James told them, struggling to catch his over-excited breath. 'Everybody, including Rosie herself, was taken by surprise. They never heard nor saw a thing, so they must have moved like ghosts.'

Jerry looked at Henry, raising his eyebrows, and giving him a "told you so" look. 'We half expected it to have taken place last night,' Jerry said. 'We were followed back here again yesterday evening by the same men who have been hounding us all week. They swaggered in here at absolute ease with themselves, totally unaware that we've been on to them from day one. There were only half a dozen travellers staying over for the night, but we still had Jack at the ready to tell them there were no vacancies if they asked for a room, just to make sure they went on their way. We then made ourselves scarce and took to our rooms to avoid any contact with them.

'Soon after, they asked for their horses and took their leave. Jack thinks they didn't have any intention of staying any longer than they did. He'd been keeping a watchful eye on them all evening and noticed that one of them was constantly glancing at his watch, and it was he who made the decision to leave at the time they did. I'll wager you, they're the men who cleared the house this morning. I just know it. All we can do now is sit back and wait to see what unfolds, and hope Townsend has his finger on the trigger.'

Henry looked at his friend with an optimistic squint and tilt of the head, thinking intensely before reeling off what he had to say. 'I have a good feeling about this. It's common knowledge that Townsend despises Caplin. I remember how Caplin was responsible for the arrest of Obo Masters, the Carlisle highwayman. He made the grave mistake of attempting to unload some of his booty into the hands of an untrustworthy pawnbroker, who instantly recognised the stolen goods because they had been listed on a broadsheet he had in his possession.

'He immediately informed Caplin rather than the authorities, because Caplin was offering a far more substantial reward, specifically to enhance his reputation. The story has it, as Obo Masters had his cruel sentence passed upon him, Caplin stood there grinning from ear to ear like a Cheshire cat. Obo then stared at Caplin with the most venomous of stares, telling him that before he meets him in hell, he'll haunt him, and all the bad things that happen to Caplin in the remaining years of his life will be down to Obo's doings from beyond the grave. He told Caplin they'll happen and sooner rather than later.

'Obo was then taken away and half hung, before being placed in chains whilst still breathing and gibbeted on a small hill by the side of the road. His tormented groans of agonising pain and desperation could be heard, much to the upset and disgust of passing travellers with their children. They looked on in bewilderment and horror, trying their damnedest to understand how such unnecessary cruelty could be found acceptable within a society deeming itself to be so civilised. He hung in that agonising state for several days until, of all people, a coachman who passed by on a regular basis could no longer bear to hear his sad, haunting, tortured groans. He decided to end his suffering with a shot to the head.

'After the trial, Caplin returned to London with his reputation as a fearsome thief-taker accomplished, and upon a chance meeting with John Townsend, boastfully told him that the only way to eradicate the criminal vermin is by hanging or transporting them. This apparently filled Townsend with indignation, for he couldn't conceive how Caplin could say such things, placing himself on the same level of integrity and good standing as that of his own. I think John Townsend has been waiting and hoping for such an opportunity to arise for some time, so he could expose Caplin for what he really is, and to do just that to Caplin himself – hang or transport him.'

Dick Ferguson sat back in his chair, one foot resting lazily on a stool, semi-engaged in the conversation taking place in front of him. 'What about Rosie?' he asked. 'She'll soon be out on the street without a roof over her head. That's a cold lonely feeling that is. Fortunately for me, I was left my father's inheritance, which helped see me through, but she appears to have no more than the clothes she's standing in.'

Jerry's eyes swept around the table with an agitated look, astounded by the hand-picked words that had drifted his way. 'Your situation can't be compared to that of this Rosie girl,' he told Dick. 'Yours was self-inflicted, but this girl's done nothing wrong.'

'Listen,' said Henry, interrupting the inevitable lecture that was about to ensue and take precedence over the conversation. 'Rosie must be looked after and treated like a princess. She's our only link to John Townsend. Billy must go and speak to her and put her mind at rest. We don't want her to think Townsend's the only one in her corner. Make her aware that you're there for her at all times, Billy. Tell her to go and find herself some lodgings that suit her needs, the nearer to Union Hall the better. Inform her that her rent will be covered in advance for one month at a time, and she'll not want for a single thing.

'When she's settled, she must make her way over to Union Hall and make John Townsend aware of her new address. If she needs to make contact with you, she must go and see Wolf Winterman at his brandy shop, and leave a message, but make her aware not to utter a word to him, for he'll undoubtedly try to wheedle out of her what's going on. You can drop by his shop daily to find out if she's been in contact. You mustn't take it upon yourself to visit her at her lodgings. Not ever. Do you understand?'

Wolf Winterman's Brandy Shop
28 May 1795, 11.15 am

THE FAMILIAR welcoming chime of Wolf Winterman's shop bell rang out above its door as Billy entered, to be confronted with the repugnant sight of Wolf devouring a meat pie.

'Your day's finally come, young man,' said Wolf, spraying the remnants of his half-eaten snack across his highly polished shop counter. 'Your little pretty one left a message with me earlier this morning. You must meet with her at the usual place, wherever that may bleeding be, at midday sharp.'

Wolf smirked broadly, exposing the mangled remains of his meal, which lay trapped grotesquely in the gaps of his teeth. 'You'd better get your arse over there my ol' son. She looked like she'd just found a penny, then lost a pound.'

At 12.08, Billy and James entered through the gate of the small, impeccably kept garden at Leicester Square, where they saw Rosie seated on one of its many benches, waiting patiently for their usual, unpunctual appearance.

'Is it possible that just for once you might make an appearance on time?' Rosie complained. 'What's the matter with the pair of you? Don't you own a watch between you?' Billy looked at James, battling to conceal his amusement.

'You sound just like a friend of ours, Rosie,' said Billy, his voice trembling on the border of an uncontrollable giggle.

'Maybe that friend of yours is getting as tired of your late appearances as I am,' snapped Rosie, refusing to share in their childlike amusement. 'One of Mr Townsend's officers of the peace visited me yesterday evening. They've arrested the men who cleared Miss Forster's house. They also arrested their accomplices. I have to go to see Mr Townsend next Tuesday, to make preparations for the evidence I have to give for him in court. That's all I've been told. The officer told me not to worry myself unduly, for it's not me that's on trial. I'm on the side of the law. He then told me it's of great interest to all concerned that I should not repeat any of what I've just been told until I've spoken to Mr Townsend.'

London Assizes
5 June 1795

JUST EIGHT days later, John Townsend was addressing the court at the London Assizes.

'The house, my lord, is situated in the middle of Castle Street, just off Leicester Square. Its only access is from the front and the rear. My officers had been keeping a vigilant watch from both ends of Castle Street, from which you can easily view the comings and goings of those who visit the property. It was from the corner of Green Street and Castle Street at 4 am, Saturday, 16 May, that my officers observed two smartly dressed men approach, turn into Castle Street and make their way with haste to the home of Miss Catherine Jane Forster, whereupon they entered the property by way of the front door with a key that they had in their possession.

'Moments later, yet another two men approached the house, following in the very same footsteps as those of the men who had already entered the house. After a short period of time had elapsed, four and a half minutes to be precise, the front door was opened and one of the men emerged from within and beckoned a carriage that was waiting at the far end of Castle Street, where it adjoins Bear Street. The carriage instantly responded to his signal and made its way to the front of the house. It was noticed that the horses' hooves had been carefully bound in sacking, a common ploy used by smugglers to quieten the horses' movements when moving their contraband under the cover of darkness.

'The front door of the house was then opened once more, and items from the house were taken and placed inside the waiting carriage. This procedure was carried out very swiftly by use of boxes and sacks. Two of the men who had been in the house then climbed into the carriage and departed. The two other individuals then brazenly returned to the house, yet again entering through the front door and proceeded to open one of the basement windows from within, leaving it slightly ajar, obviously to give the impression that this was the place of entry by the thieves, before closing the front door behind them and departing on foot in the direction of Green Street.

'Arrests were made shortly afterwards of the men who made their way on foot. The carriage itself was followed, whereupon I might add, it brazenly trotted past the home of Sir Benjamin Tebbs, our good sheriff of London, before it met up with Mathew Caplin at the location of Long Acre, St Martin-in-the-Field, a stone's throw from Mathew Caplin's residence in King Street, Covent Garden. Caplin was alone with his own personal carriage.

'The sacks and boxes containing the items from the house were then transferred again at great speed into Caplin's own carriage. It was at that moment that my officers moved in and arrests were made. I think it safe to say they were caught red-handed. And it must be said, your honour, that we were informed of this criminal conspiracy by the brave actions of a young lady who worked within Miss Forster's domestic household. We're truly indebted to her, for it was her good self who overheard two of Mathew Caplin's men utter his name and discuss the removal of the goods, and I don't use the words "his men" loosely, for they've been on his payroll for a good number of years.'

Rosie then gave her word for word account, which had been rehearsed beyond all possibility of a wrong word being spoken. As she spoke, Mathew Caplin's realisation that he'd been set up became all too clear. 'Avershaw,' he murmured between gritted teeth, clenching his fists. 'Fucking Avershaw!'

Catherine Jane Forster was then called to the witness box for questioning by John Townsend. 'Miss Forster, do you recognise the man in the dock to the left of you?'

'Yes, he was employed by my late fiancé's father, George Stokes, who is also now deceased, to bring to justice the man who robbed their home.'

'When did you last have contact with Mr Mathew Caplin?' asked Townsend.

'I have never spoken to him at any time. Never. I saw him in court during the trial of the men who were brought to justice but as I have already said, I have never met nor spoken to him.'

'Interesting,' retorted John Townsend, as he sifted with slow precision through his immaculately prepared notes. 'Are you sure you don't wish to retract that statement, Miss Forster? After all, we can all have shortfalls with our memories from time to time.'

'What are you trying to imply, sir,' came Miss Forster's somewhat agitated and nervous reply.

'Well, Miss Forster, I'm making it abundantly clear to all and sundry in this court of law that you deny having any contact with Mr Mathew Caplin. I'm not implying anything. I function only on facts, Miss Forster, nothing else.'

'Well, let me repeat it to you, sir, once again. No, I have never had any contact with Mr Caplin.'

'Well, Miss Forster, I beg to differ, you see. After I was approached by the young member of your very own domestic staff, who we have here before us, and told of the two men acting suspiciously at your home, with the name Mathew Caplin being brought to our attention through their overheard conversation, I decided to go back to school as it were and do my homework on yourself and likewise, Mr Caplin. My surveillance team, picked by my own hand I might add, excelled themselves, for you were seen in the company of Mr Caplin at the Vauxhall Pleasure Gardens, drinking soft drinks and engrossed in conversation with him for over one hour on Thursday, 14 May, between the hours of 1.00 pm and 2.15 pm. So, we for the time being have discovered at least one little lie haven't we. Your father, Miss Forster…tell me, what does he do for a living?'

'My father, sir, is a very sick man. He is not here and nor is he relevant to this case.'

'Oh, I beg to differ, Miss Forster, for as I told you earlier, I've been a good boy and painstakingly done my homework. Your father James Forster was the partner of a gentleman by the name of Albert Groves, was he not? Does this ring any bells with anyone within this courtroom? Yes, yes, of course it does, but for those not so familiar, let me enlighten you about these names.

'James Forster and Albert Groves were the sole proprietors of Forster and Groves flour mill in Southwark. You couldn't miss it, for it was a large formidable building, perched on the edge of the Thames, and it could be seen by day belching out smoke and noise. Come to think of it, for most of the night as well for that matter. It was the first steam-powered mill in the land, employing many local people, although it has to be said it put many of the smaller local mills out of business. Nevertheless, this was your father's factory, is that correct, Miss Forster?'

John Townsend awaited a reply, which eventually came. 'Yes, that is correct,' replied Catherine Forster between tightened lips.

'Ah. Now we're making progress,' announced Townsend. 'We are indeed getting somewhere. An unfortunate accident took place at that mill one cold winter's night, did it not, Miss Forster? That night being 8 December 1794, whereupon the mill was totally destroyed, ravaged by fire, apparently caused by a lack of grease on a corn machine in front of the kiln. Is that correct, Miss Forster?'

'Yes, that is correct,' came the subdued reply.

'My, my, we're moving along swiftly now,' continued Townsend. 'Progress is for sure being made. And after doing some more wonderful homework, I found that your father and Mr Albert Groves would have been sole beneficiaries from that insurance policy in the event of a terrible fire, but unfortunately that wasn't to be, was it? And why wasn't that to be? It wasn't to be due to the fact that he and Mr Groves had failed to renew their expired insurance policy for some unknown reason or other. Is this correct? And am I correct in saying that this awful tragedy rendered your father, and the rest of your family for that matter, financially insolvent?'

'Yes, that is correct.'

'This horrific chain of events, which undoubtedly played havoc with your finances…oh, wait for just one moment…I seem to be running ahead of myself and overlooked the possibility that you may have an ongoing income from elsewhere. Please enlighten me, Miss Forster.'

'I have no income from elsewhere,' came the reply.

'I know, Miss Forster. I'm well aware that you have no further income, for as you may have already guessed… yes, I did my homework yet again. Ah, progress, progress. Now think, Miss Forster, think very, very carefully indeed before you answer my next question, because total honesty will be the decisive key to helping yourself. When Mathew Caplin ordered his men into your home to remove all items of significant value, including your strongbox containing your abundant collection of fine jewellery, it was to prevent the inevitable happening, was it not? You knew that your creditors were breathing heavily down your neck and it was only a matter of time before they came and collected what was now rightfully theirs. But the frightful thought of being left destitute was just all too much for you, was it not?

'So, you made the desperate decision to call in Mathew Caplin, using, I might add, the powers of your beauty and charm to play upon his heartstrings like a harp and, of course, hatch a devious plan. Unlike your father, you made sure you had an up-to-date house insurance policy to cover your valuables, did you not? And, may I say, your little scheme was ticking along merrily, just like clockwork, for as I observed your cosy little encounter at the Vauxhall Pleasure Gardens, it looked to me like our Mr Caplin's lust for the Covent Garden bagnios[2] had, for the time being at least, dwindled somewhat, having found a woman that could without question hold his attention.'

John Townsend paused and gave a wry smile as he glanced towards Mathew Caplin. 'Yes, Mr Caplin, I did my homework yet again. But you were more than aware of this factor, weren't you, Miss Forster? You knew all too well that this man had eyes for you, and you were also aware that by taking advantage of this fact, there would be a very good chance that you would stay united with much of your wealth and splendour. This plan was to make it look as if you'd been robbed by opportunistic vagabonds, who had entered your property by a downstairs window that had accidently been left ajar by an incompetent member of staff, is that correct?'

Catherine Forster stared through John Townsend as if in a mesmerised trance, so he repeated his question. 'Is that correct, Miss Forster?'

The courtroom fell silent to the extent one could have heard the drop of a pin. 'Yes, that is correct,' came the reply.

******

After all the evidence in the cases against Catherine Forster and Mathew Caplin had been heard, Judge Fielding passed sentence on Miss Forster.

'Catherine Jane Forster, unlike your conspiring partner Mathew Caplin in this deplorable, fraudulent crime, I believe you were solely motivated by fear of being rendered destitute. Nevertheless, you did deliberately conspire to defraud your insurance company, and in doing so used every cunning and conniving means available to dupe Mathew Caplin into conspiring with you, and for this you cannot be forgiven and must pay the penalty for such actions.

I am not going to waste any further time on you, for the sentence I am about to bestow, in conjunction with the humiliation to yourself and the destruction of your family's previous good character are punishment enough. You will be taken to Marshalsea prison, where you will serve a sentence of two years, and all items retrieved by John Townsend and his officers of the peace will

---

[2] Brothels

be placed into the hands of your creditors to cover your outstanding debt. Take her away.'

As Miss Forster was being taken away, the turnkey whispered in her ear, 'Fear none, missy. You're being well looked after by your partner in crime Mr Caplin. It looks like he's already planned ahead for your little spell of special treatment, for he has a worthy gent already in deep discussion over the cost of keeping you away from the scourge of society.' The turnkey laughed as he guided her by the arm into the holding cell, closing its creaking wooden door behind him, leaving her alone with her confused thoughts of uncertainty.

Back in the courtroom, the judge moved on to Mathew Caplin, the thief-taker. 'Mathew Caplin, by chosen profession you became a thief-taker, a person who is expected to work within the boundaries of the law of the land, conducting oneself with integrity and dignity, for you were privately hired by victims of crime to bring to justice those responsible. You also, I must let this be known, collected many a bounty from the capture of criminals for the British government. This, I must say, is the part that sticks in my throat more than anything else. Your dishonesty does, in my eyes, leave an element of grave doubt, making one wonder how you conducted your past apprehensions, for you have now been proven to be a corrupt and calculating individual of irrepressible felony, who misused your position of power and authority to exploit those far less fortunate than yourself.

'This to my mind makes your actions even more deplorable. It is abundantly clear that you and Miss Forster were the sole perpetrators in a conspiracy to defraud for personal gain. Therefore, without remorse, I pass sentence upon you to be incarcerated within the confines of Newgate Prison to await your deportation upon one of our next fleet of convict ships that are bound for the Australian continent, whereupon you will serve a sentence of seven years hard labour in the penal colony of New South Wales.'

Mathew Caplin eyed John Townsend as Judge Fielding passed sentence, ignoring the judge's disapproving lecture on his unlawful activities, instead wagging his finger and nodding his head in a "this won't be forgotten" promise at Townsend.

John Townsend stared back at him with stern unadulterated composure, pronouncing to Caplin within his own thoughts: *Your hypocritical preaching of morality, when nobody dared to contradict you, have now come to a sticky end. Your glares of intimidation have no effect on me, or anyone else for that matter. Your time has come, sir, so enjoy your journey to a far-flung land, which, in my eyes, isn't far enough away to be from the likes of yourself.*

As Caplin was led away, Rosie looked at John Townsend, who, in turn, looked back at her with a confident, comforting smile as he walked over to talk to her. Her face, which had drained white throughout the proceedings, began to regain some of its colour. Her trembling, clammy hands trembled less than they had.

'Don't you worry none, Rosie from Shoreditch, the worst is over. You'll not have to set eyes on these people ever again. As for Mr Caplin, he's the one who scares you some, is he not?'

'Yes, sir,' said Rosie nervously. 'Very much so.'

'Well, like so many before him, he'll follow the same path and settle over there once his sentence has come to an end,' Townsend assured her. 'He'll undoubtedly have plenty of time to take stock, cogitate on his circumstances and come to the realisation that there would be nothing for him here anymore should he return. And as for his henchmen who were caught alongside him, they'll all suffer much the same fate when their cases are heard. Oh, by the way, come along to my office tomorrow afternoon. I have some good news for you.'

Police Office, Union Hall
6 June 1795, 2 pm

'MY MOTHER had a short spell as an actress before I was born,' Rosie began to explain to John Townsend, as they were sitting his office, 'and she hinted to me that my father was possibly a musician, but that was as far as the conversation ever progressed, Mr Townsend. I tried in vain on many an occasion to unpick the mystery of who my father was, but as time passed by, I came to the realisation that she didn't really have a clue, so alas, my father I don't know.'

Rosie sighed, resigned to the sad acceptance that her father could be no more than a fictitious image in her imagination, before continuing her tale. 'And my mother, well she's a courtesan. As I came of age, I realised that the only thing we had in common was that she was my mother. I loathed the thought that people looked upon me as Emily Hopkins's little girl and that I wasn't my own person, but the bastard child of an eccentric courtesan, so to avoid being looked upon as the daughter of a prostitute, I made the decision to move on.

'I can't deny that it hurt her deeply. It cut her to the bone, it did, so I do keep in touch with her, albeit only once in a while. She only lives in South Molton Street. Do you know, Mr Townsend, the day I left home I made up my mind that I'd never take one penny from her hand ever again. I suppose if I had I wouldn't be in this awful predicament.' Rosie laughed. 'It looks like I'm just as stubborn as she is.'

'Would you say your mother is a bit of an extrovert, Rosie?' asked John Townsend, as he poured her a soft drink.

'I think that would be safe to say,' replied Rosie with a chuckle.

'Is your mother a slave to the gin, Rosie?'

'Oh no, Mr Townsend, she usually only drinks Ratafia[3] for some reason. That is her favourite tipple.'

'What do you believe motivated her down the path to which she so sadly took herself?' Townsend asked.

'I can't really say, sir, but I know she likes the comforts and independence it brings. Heh, if you can call it independence. She's mentioned this on many an occasion, but at what cost, eh, Mr Townsend? Day in and day out making herself available for the satisfaction of male lust. I don't think so. That's not for me, I can tell you; that's why I'm taking my chances.'

Townsend smiled compassionately. 'Do you know, Rosie, I've discovered many a thing about this strange race we cohabitate amongst, and as each and every year passes by, I still find myself learning. People never cease to shock and amaze me. But your situation, I might tell you, isn't uncommon, so don't demean or isolate yourself over it, for it's not only you who carries these feelings. You know something?' Townsend went on.

'Many a courtesan lives a double life, swanning around and socialising with high society and the more affluent and prosperous of our community, many of whom deserve their place in that privileged world and, of course, there's more than a fair share of individuals that do not. It's these types that, without hesitation, pay a courtesan such as your mother handsomely to share her company, and, of course let's not overlook their outrageous earning capacity that can quadruple the average man's yearly earnings if wished. Yes, if the market wasn't there, they wouldn't be doing what they do, so ask yourself this one fundamental question: who's exploiting who? It looks to me as if it's six of one and half a dozen of the other.'

Rosie smiled, acknowledging Townsend's kind attempt to justify her mother's profession and to place her under a more endearing light.

'I'm also of the understanding that many courtesans can be very egotistical and that, of course, can make for uncomfortable living circumstances within the home if, of course, you're of the nature as one such as yourself,' explained Townsend.

'And how do you assess my nature, Mr Townsend?' Rosie asked inquisitively.

'You're a young and intelligent woman, of that I have no doubt, but that's not to say you're beyond the grasp of exploitation by characters who don't at

---

[3] A strong alcoholic almond-flavoured cordial.

first instance come across as being of the same intellect as yourself. Intelligence, common sense and worldly knowledge make for a complex mix of a human being, and it takes time, much time, for a person to get close to gaining all three and becoming that little bit more rounded. It takes years of socialising amongst the different classes in life, placing oneself in that person's shoe's as best you can before you can even begin to evaluate what motivates them. Believe me, Rosie, it's far from heaven out there.'

John Townsend and Rosie Hopkins both paused momentarily in thought. 'Mr Townsend,' Rosie chirped up.

'Yes, Rosie?'

'You still haven't told me how you assess my nature.'

'Oh yes, of course, please forgive me. Take myself as an example. I dare say you've wondered how I think, what makes me tick. Well, each and every one of us, as I said, are complex individuals, shaped and moulded by the things that we've experienced in our lives, be them good, bad or indifferent, and then of course there's good old-fashioned circumstance. But if you stick by this little rule of thumb that I'm about to tell you, you shouldn't wander too far off track.

'You see, I have this imaginary set of scales up here in my mind, and when I meet someone new, such as yourself, I'll indulge in some light-hearted conversation, followed by the odd, not too personal question. Nothing too prying you understand, for I don't wish to cause offence and blunt that person's feelings towards me. This may open up the chatter and tell me a little more about the person, and through the passage of time I begin to become better acquainted with this individual.

'By this time, I'll begin the process of placing all their good points on to one side of my imaginary scales and, of course, all the bad points likewise on the other. It doesn't take too long to get a good idea of who you're dealing with.'

'Fascinating, Mr Townsend. Truly fascinating. And why do you believe I could be so easily exploited, for I've never given anyone the hint of an opportunity to exploit myself?' Rosie hesitated before continuing. 'With the exception of my place of work that is, Mr Townsend, and I can assure you I was fully aware of my confounded situation there. Unfortunately, that's life. Sometimes you just can't do anything about it but wait and bide your time, and hopefully better yourself at the first given opportunity.'

As he looked into Rosie's eyes, Townsend saw an innocence that was exceedingly rare amongst someone with such an upbringing. It came across all too clear that for all her mother's alleged faults, she'd obviously taken extreme measures to shelter her. His imaginary scales had more good things about Rosie than bad.

'When you visited my office for the first time, Rosie, who sent you?' asked Townsend.

'Nobody, sir, I came of my own accord.'

'Oh, Rosie, Rosie, Rosie. I just had to drop a bad one on the other side of the scales.'

'Sorry, Mr Townsend, I don't understand.'

'Oh my, there we go again, another bad one's just dropped in,' Townsend said. 'You'd better stop right there before you outbalance all of the goods on the other side. Someone approached you Rosie, of that I've no doubt. If you feel you can't tell me for fear of reprisals, I can assure you, with hand on heart, that you'll be protected by myself personally and the law of our good king. These people will never know of this conversation, I promise you that. You'll be able to look them in the eye without any questionable thoughts.

'Arrests have been carried out and convictions have been made, but I know there's more to this than overheard whispers in that house that day when Mathew Caplin's name was conveniently mentioned. Now are you going to tell me, just between you and myself, or are these scales going to have me change my mind about you?'

Rosie sat rigidly in her chair, her hands resting on her knees, head bowed, unable to look John Townsend directly in the eye. 'I was approached by a young man of much the same age as myself as I left Miss Forster's house. He struck up a conversation with me. He could charm the birds out of the trees that one, I can tell you. He told me he and his friend had once worked for Miss Forster, but were dismissed unfairly, and they felt they had an axe to grind with her. That was all they were prepared to tell me.

'I was feeling terribly low at the time, for I'd just been tipped off by the houseboy that Miss Forster was in financial difficulties and we would all soon be out of a job, and in my case out on the street. They then asked me if anything underhand had taken place within the household lately, so I told them not that I knew of. They then told me to listen out and keep my eyes open and to let them know if anything suspicious began to take place and that they would keep in touch with me on a daily basis. They also said I'd be paid exceptionally well for any information that may be of benefit to them, whereupon they handed me two guineas and took their leave.

'They were very nice, especially Billy. James was nice too. I was more than aware I wasn't going to have a roof over my head before long, Mr Townsend. It was only but three days before two unfamiliar men visited the house. After what Billy and James had told me, I became immediately suspicious of these men and kept a beady eye open, only to discover they were looking at all things small and of value within the property. I knew this because it came to my attention that they didn't replace the items they had been looking at back into their rightful places, which frustrated me, Mr Townsend, for I like things to be just so.

'I told Billy and James of what had taken place and my information pleased them no end, and for this they rewarded me handsomely. That money eased my worries somewhat, I can tell you. They then went on to tell me in all sincerity of what they believed was taking place…that the two men were hired to clear the house on behalf of Miss Forster so she could make a claim on her insurance policy. And this was where the opportunity lay for them to take their revenge on her. How they became aware of the scam, I don't know, sir.

'They then told me to come and tell you of what had taken place, and it was made absolutely clear that I was to bring to light that I'd overheard the name of Mathew Caplin brought up in the conversation, just as I described in court yesterday. But that part didn't actually take place. The men didn't utter a single word. Billy and James told me they were certain beyond any shadow of doubt that he was behind it, and so to tell your good self a little white lie, which would undoubtedly arouse your attention, for they were aware that you didn't care for this man, and this would improve the chances of you personally investigating the allegations.'

'My, my, someone else has also been doing their homework, haven't they?' replied John Townsend, as he nipped his bottom lip between his teeth with anger. 'Well, Rosie, it looks to me as if your two friends have manipulated you for their own ends. Tell me, where did you meet with these devious characters?'

'At the small pretty gardens, just of Leicester Square. Oh, and on one particular occasion I had to leave a message to meet with them at a brandy shop close by St Pauls. It belongs to a man by the name of Wolf Winterman.' Rosie paused momentarily, before attracting Townsend's attention once more. 'Mr Townsend?'

'Yes, Rosie?'

'Why haven't you ever asked for the surnames of Billy and James? Surely these must be of great importance to you?'

John Townsend suppressed a giggle over such naivety. 'No, Rosie, their names will undoubtedly be fictitious. These young men aren't what they would like you to believe they are. I don't think they've ever worked for Catherine Forster. These individuals are connivers who've concocted this story to lure me into making these arrests, and have you committed perjury under oath. I know the people who were brought to justice were without doubt responsible for the crimes, and their punishment was indeed justified but, nevertheless, that little white lie that Billy and James made so light of to you was anything but. Indeed, it was one bloody great whopper.

'You must understand that these arrests wouldn't have taken place had it not been for your deceitful little story. It's safe to say that they would have had every chance of evading justice, because their arrests would have been made under fictional evidence that could have quite easily returned their freedom on a technicality.'

John Townsend suppressed his inner rage and compromised his words to no more than a mild ticking off for Rosie. He knew all too well how easy it had been for her to be seduced by these men. After all, he was still coming to terms with the reality that he'd just been hoodwinked himself, and it was a very, very bitter pill to swallow.

His concerns grew over the impact it could have on his and his officers' reputations if at any time this sorrowful affair ever leaked out. Their ability to function as highly respectable officers of the peace would for sure be heavily tarnished at best. It would be far better, he told himself, to let this newly acquired information travel no further than the four walls of the room in which it had been obtained.

His decision, without a second's consideration, was to take the route of bringing these tricksters down. Their confidence must be at an all-time high. He winced to himself, shuddering with embarrassment. Their cocky arrogant swaggers would be even more pronounced, if that were possible, as they strolled from inn to tavern, wallowing in the satisfaction of their orchestrated destruction of Mathew Caplin and Catherine Forster at his expense.

It's all beginning to piece together, he told himself. *Why else would Mathew Caplin cuss the name of London's most notorious highwayman under his breath, but for the fact that he was behind all of this?* An unnerving grin crept over the lawman's face as the realisation of Rosie's confession had placed him back in the saddle, with his foes sitting back in idle ignorance, unaware that his new findings about them had just placed the advantage back in his domain.

******

'Ah, Henry Watts. I've had a deep intriguing discussion with Sergeant Blake about this one,' explained John Townsend to his officer as he looked over his notes later that afternoon. 'Blake's had many a run-in with this one over the years, all the way back to the schoolyard of St Saviours would you believe. He described Watts as a deep calculating child, with a very reserved nature, and actions that take priority over words.

'While many a child would boast idle threats, Watts would say absolutely nothing, but carry out his vendettas without the blink of an eye. The children were quick to understand the underlying threat of one of his cold, quiet looks and gave him a wide berth. Sergeant Blake recalled that it was very difficult to fathom out how or what he was thinking and believed him to be a child of above average intelligence, although he seemed to use it for his own deep means and not for that of the classroom.'

John Townsend coughed with uneasiness as he asked his Sergeant to reveal his long-standing knowledge regarding one of the men that he was certain was responsible for his deeply inflicted wounds of humiliation.

Sergeant Blake took up the story. 'It came to light that even at this early age he'd developed severe issues with authority. He quite simply couldn't tolerate being told what to do by his teachers, or by anyone else for that matter. I also recall being told by one of Watts's tutors that for all their efforts and measures, their attempts would always end with the same sad result. They would always go full circle back to their starting point. He was sadly deemed a lost soul.

'Although he distanced himself from the majority of the children, he did strike up a friendship with a boy by the name of Lewis Jeremiah Avershaw, a boy who, in personality terms, sat at the opposite end of the spectrum to that of Watts. Chalk and cheese, you might say. But whatever their discrepancies in character, something between them clicked and they became inseparable. Their little community of villainy apparently grew from there.'

John Townsend climbed from his chair. 'Thank you, Sergeant Blake, and could you please inform the room of what you know about Mr Avershaw?'

'Yes, sir. He claims to make his living as a horse dealer amongst other things, and has a penchant for the fighting cocks, where he's been known to gamble away grand sums of money on a regular basis. He's been seen recently in the company of a man of much the same age as himself who goes by the name of Dick Ferguson, a man of which at this moment in time we know very little.

'I can, with a good degree of certainty, say that the partaking of such a gambling pastime can account for many of his acts of criminality that we believe take place upon our king's highway, no less to feed his insatiable habit. It's also worth noting that one of his close friends, to whom he laid claim as a business partner in the horse and cattle trade, was a man by the name of Joe Lorrison, who met his fate at the gallows. This must be mentioned, for it gives clear insight into the type of company he mixes with, if there was any doubt before.

'This fellow Lorrison stood brazenly on the gallows before he was about to be turned off, and wantonly, without any sign of nerve, addressed the crowd with the words: "Now and then I would borrow a little money upon the king's highway to recoup my losses at the gambling house. Unfortunately for me, my gamble this time was another loss. Damn! What's a man to do?" He told this to the crowd with an arrogant smile. Of course, the bloody crowd loved him and cheered emphatically as he bowed and took his leave from—from this world. Unfortunately, we're in, as many of these individuals are looked upon as heroes. "Knights of the road", many call them.' John Townsend had listened alongside his men, waiting for his officer to pause for breath before he took the opportunity to interrupt him. 'May I just say, Sergeant Blake, that while we're taking measures to apprehend these men, we must be careful not to overlook the circumstances for which many of these crimes are responsible. Gambling is a major factor, as the story of Joe Lorrison clearly indicated.

'It's our duty to arrest and make examples of those responsible for misguiding our youngsters on to this ill-trodden path, particularly those who trudge up and down our streets with their orange barrows and dice, which, I grant you, may seem petty and irrelevant at first sight. But when viewed with a more educated eye, this reveals circumstances that could, and in many cases does, lead to ill consequences. These schoolchildren to young apprentices who are taught to play dice and then develop the habit and empty their pockets often take to theft of one kind or another to regain their losses.

'And let me say this. It doesn't only lay in the hands of our lower classes, indeed no. This disease can be found amongst our young clerks of our merchants, to our bankers and brokers. Right here under our noses. Indeed, many of these men can be found in gambling houses up and down the land, rubbing shoulders with the likes of Avershaw and Watts on a daily basis. And, of course, this can't be a good thing. I apologise for the interruption. Please continue, Sergeant Blake.'

'Well, sir, as mentioned earlier, Avershaw's claim to being a horse and cattle trader by profession is difficult to disprove, for he has under his wing many a sharp-witted rogue who would swear blind they buy and sell stock on his behalf. These evasive individuals would have no qualms in defending his corner. They would swarm around like bees to protect him.'

'Yes, yes, I'm sure he does have an abundance of these unsavoury characters at his beck and call. The type our good king,' here John Townsend paused to tip his hat in respect, 'refers to as from the cradle to the grave offenders. Rogues of such ill character who are entwined in a web of such deep-seated villainy that it's almost impenetrable. Watching one another's backs is their key to survival. Like a flock of wild geese, you might say. These scamps will always have a bloody alibi, but we do know one thing for certain, and that's after checking through all of Avershaw's convictions, an interesting pattern of his behaviour emerged. Yes, after doing my homework, yet again, we discovered our Mr Avershaw to be of a very hot-headed disposition, or, if you want to put it another way, he has a very short fuse. Our friend seems to have an Achilles heel.'

Police Office, Union Hall
10 June 1795

A FEW days later, John Townsend was again talking to Rosie Hopkins, having asked her to call into his office.

'This is how I see your situation at this moment in time, Rosie. You've reached that point in the road where you're unsure which way to go. If you follow the path that's incorrect, you'll end up making a time-wasting journey leading you down deeper into the dungeons of life. On the other hand, if good fortune is on your side and you take the correct path, you'll undoubtedly reach your destiny, and in all probability shape your life for the better. Now, as you may well be aware, I'm forever preaching about keeping our youth on the straight and narrow, so I decided to put into practice what I'm forever preaching and, by doing so, giving someone deserving an opportunity to better oneself in life. That can only be a good thing, don't you think?'

Rosie gave one of her familiar smiles as she listened to John Townsends's kind words. 'I think that would be a far-reaching kindness, Mr Townsend.'

'This is an opportunity to give you some direction, Rosie. A destiny,' Townsend continued. 'It can only be of benefit to you. Over the years, I've struck up relationships with some good decent people, who I'm proud to refer to as friends, and one of these good friends resides in Exeter, Devon. His name is Sir Robert Kinnear.

'Now forgive me, for I've taken a terrible liberty, Rosie, and made arrangements for you to be taken under the wing of this fine gentleman's establishment to be trained as a kitchen maid. You'll love it there, Rosie. It's called The Hotel and Sir Robert himself told me there's every opportunity of bettering yourself further if you show good sense and enthusiasm, two things I know you have in abundance. I have no doubt in my mind that if you take the offer, you'll live up to my expectations and give an excellent account of yourself.

'You'll love Exeter, Rosie. It's a wonderful city. You'd be hard pushed to find a finer environment to settle in if you searched from top to bottom. Did you know that The Hotel was the first building to be declared a hotel rather than an inn? The word is French you know. I can't understand all this French nonsense, especially with what's going on at the moment, but there you go. But that aside, this is the place to stay if you're a person of substance. It's located in a spot called Cathedral Yard, a majestic location, absolutely wonderful. It's also the business hub of the city, and most probably the whole of England come to think of it. Substantial deals are born and raised here Rosie. Would you believe it if I told you that gentlemen actually rent rooms there just to have a presence in the area? Such opulence, don't you think?'

John Townsend poured a cup of tea and placed it on the table by Rosie's side, watching as she gracefully picked it up and took a sip. He was impressed with such fine mannerisms and etiquette in one so young from the opposite side of the fence.

'As you can see, Rosie, I've given this much thought and consideration. I've once again done my homework,' said Townsend. Rosie rolled back her eyes and giggled, unable to control her amusement. John Townsend chuckled along with her.

'You're so funny. You do so make me laugh,' said Rosie with a noticeable glint of admiration in her eyes.

'I've also taken into account that you visit your mother from time to time, and this to my mind can only be a good thing. You should always be there for one another and keep in contact, and Mr Kinnear has given this consideration and kindly told me that he'll give you leave to fulfil such visits. As I said before, he's a kind man.

'From time to time, my good wife and I make the journey down to visit him and his fine wife, Davina, so we'll be watching over you to see how you're getting on. You'll have a smooth path there, so you'll not have to worry about any obstacles in your way. Davina will make sure of that for you. We, of course, will keep in touch by letter if you wish. My dear wife does love to write a letter. That's of course if you're interested.'

'I don't need to think twice about it, Mr Townsend,' said Rosie excitedly. 'I'm very grateful for all the trouble that you've put yourself through over me, so the answer is yes. There's nothing to keep me here apart from the concerns over my mother, and it seems to me, as always, you've done your homework in that department.'

John Townsend chuckled. 'I have indeed, haven't I, Rosie. Yes, I have indeed.'

'And to be quite honest with you, Mr Townsend, the thought of running into Billy and James again does bother me a little, for I wouldn't feel too comfortable in their presence, not after what I've told you.'

'I understand, Rosie,' Townsend assured her. 'That's why I thought you might like a fresh start. They're all very kind people where you'll be going. They'll make you feel at home straight away. Mr Kinnear has told me they'll be employing another young girl who lives locally, and he's informed me he'll start her on the same day as yourself, so you'll have the opportunity to strike up a friendship, and things will be a little less daunting for the two of you.'

'That sounds nice, Mr Townsend. I'm comforted by Mr Kinnear's thoughtfulness.'

'By the way, Rosie, do Billy and James know of your mother?'

'No, sir, it's not the sort of thing I'd discuss with anyone. You're the exception.'

'Good. Keep it that way.' Townsend instructed Rosie. 'Speak to your mother and inform her of your intentions. I'll make arrangements for your coach. How does next Thursday sound?'

Rosie looked at John Townsend, momentarily stunned at the pace at which things were moving, before quickly composing herself. 'That would be just fine. How exciting.'

'Good. If you're happy, I'm happy, my dear. By the way…if you're to tell your mother of your address, be sure to swear her to secrecy. There's no good reason for anyone to know of your whereabouts is there?'

'Mr Townsend, they're my sentiments entirely,' Rosie agreed.

Marshalsea Prison (The Master's Side), Southwark
13 June 1795

'MORNING, YOUNG lady,' said the turnkey in no more than a whisper, as his eyes wandered over Catherine Forster from head to toe, his smarmy thoughts of sexual desire unashamedly abandoned. 'Mr Clarke, the kind gent who's been looking out for you on Mr Caplin's behalf, has asked me to be the bearer of good news for you.' As the turnkey spoke, a strong stench of urine and excrement drifted in through the open door, causing Catherine to wince and gag, before desperately grasping at her vinaigrette and holding it under her nose.

The turnkey grinned as he continued. 'Although you have the privilege of access to the prison's open buildings, shops and restaurant, you just can't seem to rid yourself of that vile stench that forever lingers under your nose. Some of the vermin in here smell worse than a rat's rotting carcass, I can tell yah. It must be awfully difficult for someone such as you to be in such close proximity to these lice-infested individuals, especially with those long, shiny locks of yours. They simply beg infestation, don't they?

'But you must admit, life is certainly a darned sight more comfortable when you have someone with considerable influence and wealth behind you. Think of all those poor wretches who don't have such a person in their corner, struggling for survival, day in and day out on bread and water, without any hope of seeing the rising of the morning sun or catching a glimpse of the birds on the wing on a wonderful summer day. No, none of that, just forever suffering in darkness. And it must be said, missy, for far less a crime than that of your own.'

'I believe, sir, you are the bearer of good news,' said Catherine Forster abruptly, whilst brushing her hair and eyeing herself in her silver hand mirror, resisting the contemptuous glare of the man she found hard to hide her repulsion for.

The turnkey continued his line of conversation, ignoring her every word. 'Did you know that this morning, while you were deep in slumber, some poor soul who had fallen on hard times and had accumulated a small amount of debt, couldn't afford to pay me to put his leg irons on, so his debts have increased even more so. At this rate, he'll never see freedom again. It's bloody terrible what takes place within these walls. I know that if I were in your shoes, I wouldn't upset Mr Clarke, and would listen to what he had to say to me with the utmost respect.'

Catherine continued brushing her hair as she replied, 'Well, if Mr Clarke wishes to come and visit, I would of course be interested in what he has to tell me, for I am deeply indebted to him for his efforts in placing me in these so-called privileged circumstances, away from, as you so quaintly put it, those poor wretches.'

'Well, missy,' said the turnkey, sneering at her cold-hearted sarcasm, 'that's good to hear but unfortunately, Mr Clarke won't trouble himself with a visit within these murky walls because, you see, the prison is technically under the control of the Knight Marshal, and he and Mr Clarke don't see eye to eye with one another. The reason for this I don't know, but Mr Clarke, as I say, won't enter the prison grounds.

'This is why I'm here. You see, Mr Clarke and the prison governor have come to an arrangement, with much money changing hands over you my dear, so you can serve your sentence as a debtor rather than the heavier sentence that should have been dealt to you. That means you'll have access each day to work on the outside of the prison walls in a cosy little haberdashery shop, returning only in the evening to rest your pretty head. As you can see, I'm the keeper of the golden key, which will release you into the big wide world, albeit at this moment in time, only temporarily, so you can meet with Mr Clarke to discuss your new little job.

'Mr Clarke has been a close friend of Mr Caplin's for many years, and that's why he's taking care of all his business affairs and, of course, looking after you. So, you see, I think it only correct that you should meet with him, tilt your ear in his direction and listen with all sincerity to what he has to say. But before that moment arises, I must make it more than clear to you: don't get any ideas about absconding, for that wouldn't be to your advantage.

'If you play your cards right with Mr Clarke, things can be very good for you, and your time will pass far more quickly. Before you know it, your sentence will be no more than a distant memory. But if you take it upon yourself, in a moment of blind madness, to have it on your toes…well, that will put you in the position of being forever on the run, and I don't think you're the type to live forever looking over your shoulder as a way of life. What do you think missy?' the turnkey asked.

'Ease your fears,' Catherine replied. 'I can assure you that will not be happening. I intend to pass these two dark years as quickly and as comfortably as humanly possible, without any conflict. How would you people put it…keep my head down and do my time. Is that correct?'

The turnkey sneered in replying, 'Aye, that's how us people would say it, pretty one. Keep your head down and do your time.'

'So, when am I to meet with Mr Clarke?' Catherine asked.

'Next Monday, the day after tomorrow, in case you've lost all recollection of time. I'll come for you at eight o'clock sharp and give you the details of where you're to meet him. But before then he's given me this note with a street map and address of the haberdashery shop where you'll make your start within the week, if it's agreeable with you, that is. He thought it best that you meet with the proprietor and look it over for yourself. Apparently, she's a sweet old love, widowed not too long ago, by the name of Annie Hanway.

'It's a nice establishment, not too posh mind you, for Mr Clarke doesn't wish you to bump into any of your old friends or acquaintances. He's picked this place to save you any potential embarrassment. A thoughtful man is Mr Clarke, the cream of society, no question about it. He asked me to tell you that you must be there first thing Monday morning at half past eight, before the shop's open for business. It's no more than a fifteen-minute walk from here. I'm sure you'll enjoy the stroll in the fresh air. It's funny how the little things in life grow in stature once they've been taken away from you, don't you think? Remember, I'll come for you at eight, so be ready. We don't want to be late now do we?'

******

On Monday morning, the key clinked into its lock and turned slowly. Catherine Forster sat bolt upright in her chair, dressed impeccably as always, awaiting the turnkey's usual irritating words to greet her.

'Morning, missy,' he called, as he shuffled lazily through the door.

And there it is, she said to herself. *Morning missy*. She loathed everything about him. His ignorance was beyond anything she'd ever encountered before. The ignorant underclass didn't even realise when he was being offensive. She felt he shouldn't even be inhaling the same contaminated air as her. That was how wide she saw the void between them.

'Well, well, look at you all done up like a dog's dinner, ready and waiting like a good little girl for me,' said the turnkey.

'I am not a little girl, sir, and I am most certainly not waiting here for the likes of you! I have an appointment with this Mrs Hanway, and I intend to be punctual, so if you would kindly hand me the note with the map and address, I will be on my way.'

The turnkey looked at her with begrudging contempt, saying, 'I'll give you the note when I'm ready, missy, and not before. Just remember who has the upper hand here in this prison. Yes, let me remind you that you're in prison, not some fancy fucking opera house. Your little arse is at my mercy, and don't you forget it. Now come with me and don't speak until you're spoken to or you'll find there's a much darker side to this place than the one you've been seeing of late.'

The turnkey angrily spun on his heels and made his way out of the room and through the labyrinth of dingy, dimly lit, dust-ridden corridors, eventually arriving at a gate on the prison's perimeter wall. 'Now here's your map and address, missy, don't lose it or you'll be fucked.'

Catherine Forster took the note, resisting the temptation to be drawn into a battle she couldn't win with a man whose foul words were said intentionally to rile and offend.

'Now take note,' said the turnkey. 'When you leave here, you'll turn left into Angel Alley, which will then lead you to Borough High Street. When you reach Borough High Street, turn right and then use the map. You can also use the map to find your way back. Be at this gate at eleven o'clock on the dot. If you're not here, you'll be classed as an absconder, do you understand me? Have I made myself clear to you, missy?' The turnkey's tone was far more scathing than ever before.

'I'll be here at eleven o'clock this morning on the dot, sir. Thank you,' came Catherine's respectful reply, in an attempt to staunch the flow of escalating tension between them.

'Good, now be off with you,' replied the turnkey, closing the gate with a repugnant stare.

Catherine Forster walked in the direction that the turnkey had told her then paused momentarily at the corner of the street.

'You look lost, dearie,' a woman's voice said. 'Can I be of assistance to yah? I've lived around here all my life, so I'm sure I can point you in the right direction.'

Catherine continued to study her map without as much as a turn of the head to acknowledge the woman's existence. 'No, it's fine. I know where I am going, thank you.'

'Aw, don't be like that, luvvie. 'Round here it's rude to rebuff a good turn offered,' replied the woman, but Catherine Forster ignored her words and continued on her way, doing her utmost to put as much ground as possible between herself and the woman.

After covering a respectable distance to be clear of her, Catherine glanced curiously over her shoulder and saw the woman making her way slowly in the opposite direction. She was a sad, frail figure, hopping away on a solitary crutch, as she was missing the lower half of her left leg, and she was old…very old.

Catherine froze on the spot. *What has become of me? Someone shows me a kindness and I am thinking the worst of them.* She was embarrassed at her uncaring, self-centred act. *Take stock of yourself woman!* she told herself, as she continued on her way down the dusty street, looking with intense concentration at the numbers on each and every shop door. *Ninety-four, ninety-two…where the hell is Mrs Hanway's shop? It definitely says number ninety on the map. But ninety is a butchery. How can that be?*

Panic began to set in. Her hands became clammy and she began to break into a cold sweat. The clock was ticking, and she couldn't afford to be late. *What now?* she asked herself. *Everything is still closed and there is nobody around to ask.* She turned around in desperation, looking for assistance. A sense of relief flushed over her as she noticed an ageing reverend emerging from a narrow alley on the opposite side of the road.

She hurriedly made her way over to seek his help. 'Excuse me, reverend, I think I am lost.'

The clergyman turned sharply to face her, striking with all his force across her neck. Catherine fell to the ground, clutching desperately at her throat in a vain attempt to staunch the flow of blood that gushed from her gaping wound, as she eyed the glistening razor clasped in the blood-splattered hand of her sneering attacker.

'You didn't really think Mr Caplin was going to allow you to live the good life after you helped bury him in court, did yah, missy?' The smartly disguised turnkey leaned over Catherine Forster's stricken body, staring hard into her eyes as he turned his head from side to side, watching intently as all signs of life drained slowly from her dying body, plummeting her into death's never-ending darkness.

Wimbledon Common, London
17 June 1795, 8.30 pm

THE HAZY silhouettes of three men on horseback slowly drifted along the brow of a hill, unperturbed by the haunting sight of a lone gibbeted offender swinging within a cart's length of their horses.

Jerry Avershaw, Henry Watts and Dick Ferguson were tired, still partially drunk and a little bit downhearted. Much money had changed hands at the cock pit earlier in the day and it wasn't in their favour. The three men had then spent the rest of the day in the Black Bull alehouse to, as Jerry called it, "perk up their spirits a little".

Their gaming events always followed the same predictable path. If their luck was in and a profit was made, they would head straight for the alehouse to celebrate their good fortune, spending their easily earned winnings like money was going out of fashion. And if they lost? They would still go to the alehouse and…well…spend what money they had left between them to drown their sorrows. Whatever happened, be it at the cock pit, the card table or the good old boxing, it would always end the same way – riding back to the Bald Faced Stag half logically connected, and more often than not potless.

Jerry straightened up in his saddle, his attention drawn to three horsemen in the distance. 'What have we here then,' he slurred. 'Three villains or three fools?'

'I'd say neither,' said Henry, aware that his friend was far more inebriated than himself. 'They could well be officers of the law.'

Dick Ferguson looked at his friends as the horsemen drew closer. *Jerry would have known exactly who they were dealing with by now if he were sober*, he thought to himself. *That familiar spyglass would have been the first thing to leave his pocket and give him the upper hand.* It wasn't a good sign that Jerry's usual habit hadn't immediately come to mind.

'It's three soldiers,' said Dick. 'They all look like captains.'

'Well, well, three captains of the militia,' said Jerry, as he glanced at Henry and laughed, noticeably sobering, his adrenaline obviously on the march through his veins.

Dick watched as Henry cocked his pistol, then Jerry did likewise. It wasn't a good sign. Henry's sombre mood changed in an instant, as did Jerry's, and Dick watched with mesmerising fascination as his friends slipped into hunting mode, like hungry wolves fixed entirely on the visions approaching them. There was something unnatural, even creepy about the way in which their mood changed simultaneously, as if there was a little something more going on than just the combination of alcohol and hatred for authority that brought out the worst in them.

The three highwaymen's masks were pulled up over their weather-beaten faces instinctively as they closed in, heads down, pistols at the ready. They hit their distance of attack like a pugilist naturally knows his distance from which to impose his heavy punches.

'Damn your eyes, stop!' growled Jerry, as he engaged the captain nearest to him. Venomous glares were exchanged between the two men. The captain cut a small insignificant figure, one could even say remotely fragile, but his looks were deceiving as he spoke with a cocksure confidence that bordered on the arrogant.

'Do not cross us. Be on your way or the repercussions for your actions will be immeasurable,' said the captain scornfully.

'I can see that you look upon us with the highest esteem, gentlemen,' said Henry sarcastically.

Dick watched as Henry's horse showed unusual discomfort at being in such close proximity to that of the captain's. He smirked under his mask. *Even their steeds dislike one another. Such bad chemistry…cats and dogs*, he thought to himself. *Cats and dogs!*

Police Office, Union Hall
20 June 1795

JOHN TOWNSEND sat at his desk pondering where on earth to start first. He wasn't relishing the task of catching up on the vast backlog of work he'd accumulated during his time-consuming battle with Joseph Caplin. But in his mind's eye he knew it had been worth going that extra mile to bring Caplin to justice and remove him from an ever-expanding, exploitative position of power, which, if not harnessed, would have led to grave problems for himself further down the line. *Sometimes you have to remove the rot before it contaminates everything around it*, he thought to himself.

He was feeling pleased with his success, albeit with the embarrassing moment here and there, when his concentration was broken by a gentle knock at his door. He ignored it but it was followed by yet another, just as gentle, almost apologetic.

'Oh, come in!' Townsend said, feeling exasperated. 'You're obviously not going to go away.'

The door opened. It was Corporal Boare. Townsend smiled, slightly embarrassed after realising who it was. Corporal Boare was a heavily built man, quietly spoken and very level headed. He took no nonsense from anyone, but his nature was such that he rarely had to go down the road of chastising anyone for slights. He could have climbed the ladder within the force, without question, but chose not to. He liked where he was, out there communicating with the public. He was a very helpful man, who rarely had a bad word spoken about him, which was quite some achievement within his line of work.

'Sorry to interrupt you, guv, but we've just been informed of a robbery that's taken place on Wimbledon Common late yesterday evening. I had to ask them to repeat what they told me because I couldn't believe my ears the first time around. The men who were robbed were three captains of the militia.

As I'm telling you I still can't believe it...not one captain, not two captains, but three, and they're adamant it was Jerry Avershaw and two other assailants.'

'What proof do they have that it was Avershaw, Corporal? Did they see his face? Did he leave a calling card? What? Enlighten me.'

'No, guv, nothing like that. They said they were approached by three men so full of audacity that it couldn't have been anyone else. They won't let this go, guv. They're spitting blood.'

'I think we should make arrangements to have a little chat, don't you, Corporal?' suggested Townsend.

'Captain Hall, guv,' said Corporal Boare. 'He's the man to speak to. It's Captain Hall of the 38th Foot.'

'Yes, yes, let's speak to this Captain Hall of the 38th Foot and find out why he so adamantly believes it to be our Mr Avershaw,' replied Townsend.

Corporal Boare immediately went away to make the necessary arrangements and Captain Hall appeared at John Townsend's office the following morning at 9 am.

'Good morning, Captain,' Townsend greeted his visitor. 'I'm glad you could make it this morning. I'm fully aware that you're a very busy man, so I appreciate you giving me your precious time.'

'As you are aware, Mr Townsend,' said the captain, launching straight into business, 'Captain Peregrine, Captain Holt and I suffered a grave indignity at the hands of three armed villains. Firstly, I would like to thank you for keeping this unfortunate episode as low key as one possibly could, at least until we remove this man Avershaw and his cronies from the world in which they live.' Captain Hall scratched at his chin and paced the office floor.

'I agree implicitly, Captain. These men must be brought to justice, but tell me, why are you so sure it's Jerry Avershaw?' asked Townsend as he poured a brandy and handed it to his visitor.

'Observation is as important an ingredient in your line of profession as it is in mine, is it not?' the captain said. John Townsend nodded emphatically in agreement, as the captain continued his tale of events. 'The three men who dared to rob us were heavily intoxicated. They stunk to high heaven of ale. It was a chance hold up with liberties taken. The mannerisms with which they approached us told me they were not fresh-faced chancers. No, of that I am certain. Have you ever seen a pugilist from the amphitheatre involved in an unpaid brawl in a tavern, Mr Townsend?'

'No, I can't say that I have.'

'Well, sir, I have witnessed such an event, if that's what you would call it, and trust me, they stand out like a sore thumb. The punches come from all angles with devastating precision, while the other chap flounders and looks rather ridiculous. It is all over very quickly, thank goodness. What I am trying to say is that these deplorable characters, although under the influence of alcohol, were veterans. It stood out to me as clear as the pugilist in the tavern. No doubt about it. My fellow captains were of the same conclusion.

'I noticed that one of the men was rather more reserved and held back more so than the other two. He seemed more hesitant, not so familiar with the highwayman's ways, but I can assure you that if he is an apprentice, he will learn bloody quickly with that pair. He was the one that was ordered to take our pistols and valuables. They cheekily let us keep our swords, warning us that if we should get all hot-headed and pursue them, sword in hand like crazed brigands, they would "fucking shoot us up our arses".'

John Townsend placed his clenched fist over his mouth and coughed, in an attempt to stifle the result of an image he'd so childishly concocted in his head.

The captain continued. 'I have not seen such simmering hate for some time and, believe me, I have seen some in my time. These men were as bad as it gets. That was Avershaw alright, and that other bastard in his company…'

'Was probably Henry Watts,' interrupted John Townsend in his usual manner. 'Yes, Captain, I've been doing my homework.'

'I am pleased to see you have names, sir,' said Captain Hall. 'I am not in the habit of asking the Runners to solve military problems, but I understand that you must be informed, and our weapons must be returned. Our embarrassment will sink to an even lower depth if it be found that our weapons were used against our aristocracy or the general public to extract their belongings. These culprits must be apprehended and punished accordingly. If you do not move with haste in this direction, you may well find that we have beaten you to it.'

'I understand completely the significance of your situation, and that of your fellow captains,' Townsend assured him. 'And I agree, this must be dealt with fast and furiously. I'll seek a warrant for the arrest of Watts and Avershaw, so we can get them in for questioning as soon as possible.'

'I appreciate your efforts, Mr Townsend,' replied the captain gratefully. 'As I said, our pistols must be back in our possession at all costs. One more thing, sir...as these men relieved us of our weapons, they sent us on our way with the words "now be off with you", laughing as they said it. They held fast, unlike other highwaymen and footpads, who usually rob and flee. They were not going to be the first to take flight, as if sending a message of power and control. If it was not Avershaw and this man Watts, then who the hell were they? Whoever they are, they are now at war with the military.'

******

John Townsend's mind was racing as he sat in his office later that day. He began to feel anxious. The taking down of Avershaw was by no means going to be a walk in the park. He also knew he had the full weight of the military bearing down heavily on his shoulders. His line of thought took a turn in direction. He had so many questions to ask himself, the main one being why Mathew Caplin had murmured those dark oaths under his breath about Avershaw.

Maybe, just maybe, our man Avershaw knew that Caplin had an inkling that he was at the home of George Stokes on the evening of the robbery and, if this was the case, he would of course be of the mind that Caplin and Forster weren't going to let things drop until they met with their comeuppance. If so, Avershaw would certainly fight fire with fire. He was far too astute to roll with things and hope that it may all fizzle out, as he more than understood Caplin's tendencies to work either within the confines of the law or outside of it when necessity came calling.

Parts of the jigsaw were beginning to slot into place for John Townsend. The sooner he could obtain a warrant the better his chances of hunting Avershaw down and pulling him in for questioning about the highway robbery of the three captains on Wimbledon Common. Then at the same time he could probe him over the Stokes robbery and maybe, with a little luck, Avershaw might trip himself up under the onslaught. *We know he's cunning but how good is his memory? Let's hope that by hook or by crook we can retrieve those bloody pistols*, thought Townsend.

As he sat pondering his options, Townsend began to think out loud. *Probable cause...we need a level of reasonable belief based on facts. We couldn't present only the three captains' assumptions to have a warrant granted, so we must dig deeper, but how?* His anxiety grew as he leant over his desk, holding his head in the palms of his hands, engrossed in deep thought.

A genteel knock on the office door resounded around the quiet of his room, relieving him of his moment of anguish. 'Come in, Corporal Boare,' said Townsend, guessing correctly at the familiar knock from his officer.

'I hope you don't find my intrusion inappropriate at this moment in time guv,' said Corporal Boare. 'I know you're up to your eyes in it, but I think I may have some newly acquired information that may be beneficial to you.'

'Do continue, Corporal. I think I need all the help I can get,' replied Townsend despondently.

'Well, guv, while I was out and about doing the rounds yesterday evening, I was told of some gents making their way to the theatre with their wives whose carriage had apparently been restricted from making its way to the front of the building by four men mounted on their horses who were engaged in conversation with two other men on foot. The men were asked to move aside by the occupants of the carriage, but they wouldn't budge an inch and an argument ensued, resulting in one of the gents disembarking from the carriage to remonstrate with one of the men who had rather more to say than the others, much to the amusement of his friends.

The ruffian then dismounted from his horse and punched the gent hard in the face, breaking his jaw. This apparently amused his cronies even further. The unfortunate victim was a Doctor Harper. I think you have the problem of the warrant solved guv, because there were no masks worn on this occasion,' said Corporal Boare with a cheeky twinkle in his eye.

'My, my, life is full of surprises, eh, Corporal; sometimes bad, sometimes good. Do you fancy a nice cup of tea?' Corporal Boare smiled and pulled up a chair. 'So, it was just pure coincidence that you were in the vicinity of Lewis Jeremiah Avershaw and were told of the incident by some helpful soul who bumped into you by chance as you walked your beat, placing you in a position to assist the distressed doctor. Is that correct?'

'Well, guv, over the years I've helped many a person and many a family with all kinds of problems, and they know that if I'm told anything it won't go any further. They trust me not to put their names out there and I'm proud to say I never have and never will. I help them and they return the favour, so everybody's happy. I happened to mention to one or two people that I was interested in the whereabouts of Jerry Avershaw, and the rest was pure coincidence and a little bit of good fortune.'

'So, you were just fortunate to be close at hand. Is that correct?' asked Townsend.

A smile of contentment ran over Corporal Boare's clean-shaven face as he sipped his tea. 'Yes, guv, I just happened to be in the vicinity at the time. What luck, eh?'

John Townsend didn't believe for one moment that he'd been given the full story by his officer. Good old-fashioned common sense told him there was more to this story than his corporal was prepared to reveal. He was pretty much certain that his officer had been watching Avershaw from a safe distance for some time, waiting in the wings for his short fuse to materialise into one of his notorious, predictable explosions, so giving him his golden opportunity.

Corporal Boare was protecting the people who gave him his information, and rightly so. Townsend thought to himself that this had worked meticulously for him over the years and he was certainly not going to meddle in such a well-oiled machine that worked and worked well. Good policing, yes, very good policing indeed. Townsend wished that many more of his officers had such a good relationship with the public.

'Do you think this doctor and his party will stand by their statements, Corporal?' asked Townsend.

'Yes, guv, they come from Bury St Edmunds in Suffolk and are unaware of who Avershaw is. I have no doubt they'll stand their ground…well, for the time being at least. Whatever happens, it will give us enough time to get that warrant and get him through these doors for questioning. If by then they find out who he is and get cold feet, it won't really matter none will it.'

John Townsend beamed broadly. 'I couldn't agree more. I think it's time to go and get that warrant. More tea, Corporal?'

Corporal Boare beamed back. 'Don't mind if I do, guv.'

Townsend refilled his corporal's cup, before walking over to the door and opening it and shouting. 'Sergeant Blake!'

'Yes, guv?' came the reply.

'Can you come in for a moment? Corporal Boare will fill you in on our good news, then I want you to apply on my behalf for an arrest warrant for Lewis Jeremiah Avershaw. I expect this to go no further than between the three of us for the time being. I don't want any of this to leak out. At this moment in time I don't feel that an attempt to arrest Avershaw is on the cards, as he'll undoubtedly be expecting a call from us one way or another and will have gone to ground for a short while. I think the best option is to sit back and lull him into a false sense of security. Have himself think he's got away with assaulting this Doctor Harper fellow and, in the meantime, I'm going to take a much-needed short break.'

'Anywhere nice, guy?' asked Sergeant Blake.

'Yes, Sergeant,' replied Townsend. 'Somewhere very nice indeed. Exeter, wonderful Exeter.'

The Hotel, Cathedral Yard,
Exeter, England
23 June 1795

'MR TOWNSEND, Mrs Townsend, so good to see you. It's so good to see you!' Rosie couldn't contain her excitement as she ran towards them with outstretched arms, hugging them with the greatest of affection.

Miriam Townsend looked at her husband with a smile of relief. She'd been having sleepless nights for some time, worrying and wondering whether Rosie would settle in happily or end up dismayed, recoiling into herself and becoming solemn and lonely. She needn't have concerned herself, she realised, as she witnessed such joyful emotions. Her worst fears hadn't materialised.

'And who's this dashing young man in your company, Rosie?' asked John Townsend with the inquisitiveness of a police officer who's never off duty.

'Oh, so sorry, where are my manners,' replied Rosie. 'This is my good friend, Arthur Wilson. He's been my rock. We met only one week after I arrived here, and we've been the best of friends ever since. It was Arthur who introduced me to Exeter, and he's shown me all around the city. He's educated me so much about its history that I feel I've been living here all of my life.'

'It looks to me like Rosie has settled in well. And made plenty of friends Arthur?' Townsend asked.

'Yes, sir,' replied Arthur. 'If you're a stunningly attractive young lady, all and sundry want to get to know you and be your new best friend.'

John Townsend rocked back on his heels at such in-your-face bluntness, then smiled, detecting more than a large slice of jealousy in his words. *This young man is smitten,* he told himself, before addressing the young man in question. 'I agree to a certain extent, Arthur, but don't you think the same may apply to a handsome young man?'

'No, sir, men don't stick together like women. Men seem to carry more nomadic tendencies, and so look at other men, especially handsome ones, as a threat.'

Townsend nodded as he replied, 'Maybe women also look upon other pretty woman as a threat, as you call it, but maybe they go about the elimination of that pretty threat in a more calculating, cunning way. Have you ever looked at it from that angle?'

Arthur squinted, then smiled. 'No, sir, I haven't, but I'll take your words on board and give them some serious thought.'

'Looks don't last forever, Arthur,' suggested Townsend. 'Look at it this way. Take a nice shiny freshly plucked apple. That shiny piece of perfection is only short lived, because as time goes by its unblemished exterior begins to fade and wrinkles begin to make an unwelcome appearance. It then doesn't appear so desirable. This also happens in life, where those who are more privileged in the looks department have this raging beacon to contend with, for as time goes by they'll go the same way as that bloody apple, becoming just like the rest of us mere mortals, making their way through life pretty much unnoticed, sometimes bordering on the extent of being damned near invisible.

'All of that predominant attention that was so taken for granted in those early years when gracefully drifting along the promenade and the like, slowly over time evaporates and the reality of all those pleasantries that were so lovingly bestowed upon them day after day become less frequent, until one day…wallop…it hits them hard right between the eyes. They're now bloody non-existent. I should know; I had to struggle to come to terms with this harsh cruel reality myself, glaring hard into the mirror every morning, watching as Father Time slowly and mercilessly ravaged my good looks.'

Rosie and Arthur looked at one another, while Miriam chortled and tutted, whilst shaking her head in dismay. John Townsend's tongue was planted firmly in his cheek as he tried to stifle his childlike giggles before it all became too much, and they all burst into laughter.

'Do you live locally, Arthur?' asked Miriam, still giggling.

'Yes, I live at Rougemont House with my family. It's situated just outside the entrance to Rougemont Castle.'

'I'm familiar with the house, Arthur. It's a very fine property,' said John Townsend, recalling the time he and Robert Kinnear visited the castle. It had stuck in his mind after noticing that the house still had some of its windows blanked off because of the levying of the window tax. There was also Robert's admiration of its stunning grounds and lake that were so tastefully landscaped.

'What do you do for a living, Arthur?' asked Townsend, as he avoided Miriam's disapproving glare at his over-inquisitive police tactics so early in the conversation.

'I work for my father, sir. He's a wine merchant and partner in the Exwick wool mill. Wilson and McKenna.'

John Townsend coughed a couple of times as if to clear his throat before raising his eyebrows, clearly impressed with what he'd just been told. 'My, that company is a major benefactor to the community,' he said. 'I believe your father's company is totally responsible for greatly increasing the number of inhabitants in the area. Is that true?'

'Yes, sir, that's true. It's all good for everyone concerned, sir,' said Arthur proudly, clearly in awe of his father's achievements.

John and Miriam Townsend were delighted beyond all expectations for Rosie. It looked as if she was settling in well, which, they thought, could be the deciding factor that would save her from any possible retribution from the remnants of Mathew Caplin's vicious vindictive henchman, not to mention the manipulative attentions of Billy and James, who would like to find her to continue with their controlling ways. In John and Miriam's eyes, the longer Rosie was away from London the easier it would be for her to put down her roots in Exeter permanently.

******

Two days later it was time to make tracks back to London. The Townsends' trips to Exeter under the care of Robert and Davina always seemed to pass so quickly, and this occasion was no exception. Robert, kind as always, had given Rosie some time off to share some sociable hours with John and Miriam.

'We seem to spend more time in that coach than we do socialising with our friends,' mumbled Townsend, with a submissive shrug of the shoulders.

'Maybe next time, dear, we should stay a day or two longer and make it feel more like a holiday,' replied Miriam with an understanding smile. It was clear to see she wasn't ready to leave either.

'Yes, that makes a lot of sense. We must do that next time,' replied her husband.

After making their farewells, John Townsend turned to look at the young woman that he'd made his responsibility. 'It's with a heavy heart that we must leave you for the time being, Rosie,' he said, 'but we'll return in two or three months' time. You'll write to us I hope?'

'But of course, Mr Townsend. I wouldn't feel secure without knowing that Mrs Townsend and you are there for me. In fact, soon after you arrive home there'll be a letter for you. I'll be writing as soon as your coach rolls into motion.' Rosie gave them both a comforting hug and the Townsends climbed into the awaiting coach, which carried them off until they were no more than a distant dot on the landscape.

John Townsend stared at the vacant seat opposite him as they rocked to and fro. 'I do hope she'll be alright,' he said aloud, half questioning his own integrity and half asking for a reassuring answer from Miriam.

'Of course, she will, dear. I've never seen her so contented and at ease with herself, and we both know she couldn't be in safer hands, so put your mind at rest. We don't need any more grey hairs now do we.'

John smiled, replying, 'No, definitely not. Don't you think she's changed considerably in such a short space of time, dear? That young girl who walked through my office door not so long ago is no longer the fragile insecure child she once was. She carries herself with far more confidence these days, don't you think?'

'Yes, more confidence by far. You've done a wonderful thing for her, make no mistake. As much as she loathed her mother's lifestyle, I just can't remove the niggling thought from my head that she could just as easily have been lured down that very same path. There were people waiting in the wings to take advantage of her one way or another just as they did before. I dread to think where she could have ended up. The harsh reality of her circumstances could well have forced her to fight against all her morals and follow the same existence as that of her mother, just to put food in her belly. The struggle for survival combined with being surrounded by people in the same boat makes for a bad chemical reaction.'

John Townsend shuddered noticeably. 'Yes, yes, a deplorable thought, dear, and not healthy for one to ponder over.'

Police Office, Union Hall
27 June 1795, 4 pm

'YOU WERE right, guv,' said Corporal Boare to John Townsend.

'About what, Corporal?' asked Townsend.

'We sent a couple of off-duty officers over to discreetly run an eye over the Bald Faced Stag. Avershaw's nowhere to be seen. It looks like he and his associates have made themselves scarce.'

'I didn't expect anything less of him, Corporal,' replied Townsend. 'And I didn't think for one moment that you did either.'

Corporal Boare smiled and nodded twice. 'Yes, guv, he's resorted to type. His inbuilt survival mechanism has kicked in. He and the others will return soon enough though. After a couple of weeks or so they'll return and look upon this as a triviality, trust me.'

'Yes, Corporal, I couldn't agree more. A rabbit never strays too far from its burrow. Which of our officers would recognise our man at an instant without any shadow of a doubt?'

'Price and Turner, guv,' came the corporal's reply, without the slightest hesitation. 'Both of them have had run-ins with him over the years. Good, solid, no-nonsense men they are, even with the likes of him. They're not the type to be easily intimidated, no matter what the circumstances. Officer Windsor also knows him more than he should.'

The corporal dropped his head and a smirk appeared over his face, as if recollecting a forgotten memory. 'Yes, there's no love lost between them either.' He added.

John Townsend looked steadfastly at his corporal with a puzzled look, contemplating whether he had the strength to ask what brought such an amusing smirk to his face, but then decided to let the moment pass and get on with things.

'Good, good. At the first opportunity get them into my office. Sooner rather than later if you can.'

******

The following morning, John Townsend was pacing slowly around his office's large, oblong oak table that accommodated his fellow officers. His stern eyes were fixed on the floor ahead of each and every step he took. 'I have a warrant,' he said, with his usual air of authority, grasping the document tightly in his hand and waving it vigorously in front of himself, as if to make sure it had been noticed. 'Granted, I might add, for the arrest of Lewis Jeremiah Avershaw. Officers Price and Turner, I'm entrusting you both with the responsibility for its successful execution. I've been informed that both of you have encountered this hardened criminal several times before and this is why I'm placing the responsibility into your good hands. I have total faith in the pair of you. It's only a matter of time before he rears his head.'

The two officers traded looks of contentment, tilting their weather-beaten faces towards one another with broad grins of relish. If not for their uniforms, these two officers would convincingly pass for high tobymen themselves, but that was where the similarity ended. They clearly sat on the opposite side of the fence to the man they were about to track down and arrest.

Police Office, Union Hall
12 July 1795, 11 am

'HE'S BACK, guv,' said Sergeant Blake excitedly as he entered John Townsend's office. Townsend broke out into a smile of relief, his posture noticeably taking on a more rigid, prouder stance. His frame looked less portly and he appeared to grow an extra inch or so, as if an imaginary weight had been mercifully lifted from his tired shoulders.

Three weeks had passed since they had started looking for Jerry Avershaw, but it seemed like six, so much had the strain taken its toll. Seeds of doubt had managed to trickle into Townsend's mind. All of his policing experience was once more under severe scrutiny. Jerry Avershaw had clearly become an unhealthy obsession, just like Mathew Caplin.

Townsend gathered himself whilst counting to ten. It always seemed to work for him at times like this, helping him hold his tongue and prevent him from blurting out things he would later regret. 'Please take a seat Sergeant,' he said calmly, upon witnessing the rare sight of his officer's emotions getting the upper hand on him. 'Take your time.' He added, mumbling in a quiet, controlled manner, totally contradicting his very own inner emotions.

'He's drinking and smoking at the Three Brewers public house in Maid Lane, Southwark as we speak,' Sergeant Blake informed Townsend.

'Do you know who's in his company?' asked Townsend. 'No, guv. He arrived with Henry Watts, but Henry only stayed a short while and then departed.'

The two men turned to see who had knocked at the office door, which had been left half open due to Sergeant Blake's over-excited entrance.

'Turner and Price are here but are about to go to the grammar school of St Olave's,' Corporal Boare interjected. 'It had a break-in last night. Do you need a word with them before they go?'

Good old common sense and logic. Corporal Boare excels so well at these things, John Townsend thought to himself. 'Yes, Corporal, yes,' he replied. 'Get them in here right away.' *Little common-sense things*, he whispered to himself under his breath. He knew Turner and Price weren't going anywhere near that school until they had first spoken to him.

Many a man of far more privileged an upbringing and education than that of his corporal wouldn't have held the two officers there but would have instead sent them on their way to the school without as much as a second thought. Not so with Corporal Boare. He'd been educated at the college of life and hard knocks and graduated with flying colours. He never overlooked the seemingly miniscule things that were of profound, significant importance further down the line.

'Ah, Officers Price and Turner,' Townsend greeted the two men as they entered his office. 'We must move fast. Our man has been spotted. He's drinking in the Three Brewers, Maid Lane as we speak.'

The Three Brewers, Maid Lane, Southwark
12 July 1795, 11.45 am

'SAME AGAIN, luv,' murmured the portly middle-aged man to the young barmaid as he perched on his stool beside the ale-sodden bar, which had assaulted the elbows of his coat, staining them with dark, damp circular patches. His eyes wandered over her every movement as she poured him yet another ale. The young woman felt decidedly uncomfortable with the intensity of the unwanted attention bestowed upon her, but she needn't have worried herself, for his eyes were soon to move towards the bar's heavily chipped and splintered door as it swung open sharply. Well, look who's here, a couple of uniforms.' The man sneered, whilst squinting uncontrollably through the sudden onslaught of light that intruded upon the dark, smoke-filled room. Jerry Avershaw didn't need to take heed from his drinking partner's antagonistic words. Before a single foot had crossed the threshold, he knew who the two officers were and why they were there.

'Lewis Jeremiah Avershaw, we have a warrant for your arrest. You'll accompany us back to Union Hall.' The words of one of the lawmen fell upon deaf ears as the high toby raised himself from his chair, a pair of pistols clenched firmly in each hand, placing himself between the bar and the two officers of the peace. The lawmen stood off, eyeing the outlaw with disdain. Officer Turner glanced momentarily at the pistols of his adversary. As an ex-soldier, he recognised them as military issue. *I know where they came from*, he thought to himself.

Avershaw broke the silence. 'I'll kill the first fucker who attempts to take me, make no mistake. Turn and walk away while you can!' The three men studied each another with intense measure, waiting for the next move. Price and Turner stood firm, watching the young highwayman swaying intermittently from side to side, making his heavy consumption of ale more apparent.

The officers glanced from the corner of their eye at one another, their confidence beginning to grow. They weren't about to walk away with their tails between their legs, guns or no guns. Suddenly, without warning, the two lawmen took their chance, rushing forward, hoping to throw the outlaw off his guard with the speed and vigour of their attack.

It was a fatal miscalculation. The high toby discharged both pistols simultaneously, filling the room with a cloud of gun smoke as Turner slumped face down to the floor, blood streaming from a gaping wound to his head. The contents of the other pistol lodged deep into the stomach of the unfortunate Officer Price, sending him to the ground beside his fellow officer.

Unbeknown to Jerry Avershaw and his drinking partner, the officers were far from alone. Officer Barnaby Windsor was at hand outside the notorious drinking den with several men that he had rounded up to give assistance, who, upon hearing the shots immediately ran inside to witness the horrific scene of his fellow officers battling for life on the filthy blood-and-ale-soaked floor. Turner was holding his head, groaning in pain as blood oozed between his fingers, running down his wrists and losing itself beneath the sleeves of his coat, whilst Price lay doubled over in agony beside him, the severity of his pain etched across his distorted face.

Jerry Avershaw was finally overwhelmed by Barnaby Windsor and his men, but not before being handed another pistol by a person unknown and discharging a final shot. This time the outlaw missed his mark, the slug narrowly passing by the head of Barnaby Windsor during the violent struggle that ensued. Windsor looked over dejectedly at his comrade, David Price, who was curled up on the floor, dying slowly in a great deal of pain, his suffering lasting far longer than anyone deserved.

Croydon Assizes, Surrey
30 July 1795

THE TRIAL judge, Mr Baron Perryn, made his way to his chair, the way in which he carried himself and the pace by which it was done telling all that he didn't have to answer to anybody. It had been a long, long time since anyone had cracked the whip to make him jump through a hoop. He placed himself down with a painfully slow precision before casting his stern eyes around the crowded courtroom in a way that emphasised his authority.

The musky, unpleasant smell of the previously tried was partially suppressed by the heavy indulgence of scented flowers and herbs, randomly placed around the court, and particularly more so around the judge.

Jerry Avershaw monitored the judge and those around him as they leaned over and whispered into his ear, hands cupped over their mouths in order to prevent the slightest of chances that their words be overheard. The judge listened and nodded to their guarded whispers as he eyed the accused with his usual contempt. Both judge and accused had read the newspapers prior to the trial and Jerry was aware that they were having a field day at his expense – much of it true, much of its pure fiction.

Several familiar faces caught Jerry's attention as his eyes flickered around the room. Two figures in particular held his gaze. One was John Townsend, and Jerry sneered at the man responsible for bringing him to justice. The policeman pursed his lips smugly and avoided giving Jerry the satisfaction of eye contact. The other was the man standing beside Townsend, officer Bernard Turner. He had survived, his atrocious head wound freshly bandaged for his appearance in court.

Judge Perryn opened proceedings. 'The prisoner is charged on two indictments, firstly having at the Three Brewers public house, Maid Lane, Southwark, feloniously shot and murdered David Price, an officer of the

Police Office, Union Hall within the Borough of Southwark. Secondly, having at the same time and place, fired a pistol at Bernard Turner, another officer attached of the Police Office, with the intent to murder him.'

Mr Garrow, the leading counsel for the prosecution, opened the case to the court and jury, stating, 'The prisoner at the bar is a person of very ill repute. He was suspected of having perpetrated several felonies, and the magistrates of the Police Office in the Borough of Southwark received information against the prisoner, so they, as was their duty, issued an order for his apprehension.

'The deceased, David Price, and another officer by the name of Bernard Turner went to the Three Brewers, a public house in Maid Lane, where they understood Avershaw to be drinking in the company of others. They entered the public house and, upon seeing the officers, the prisoner appeared as if intending to resist arrest, holding a loaded pistol in each hand. He threatened and cursed the officers, demanding that they stand off, otherwise he would fire at them.

'The officers, not being intimidated by Avershaw's threats, attempted to rush in and seize him, at which moment he discharged both pistols at the same time, lodging the contents of one in the body of David Price, and with the other wounding Turner very severely to the head. Price, after languishing a few hours, died of his wound.'

After Mr Garrow's animated description of the events, showing the shocking barbarity of the confrontation, he then called four witnesses. 'Their evidence,' he stated, 'will be undeniably clear in establishing the prisoner's guilt. The jury will be able to judge from the facts presented and be able to decide on the prisoner's guilt or innocence.'

The first witness called was Bernard Turner, followed by the landlord of the public house, John Churcher, then a surgeon, and finally Joyce Cotton. All four witnesses confirmed what Mr Garrow had already presented to the court. Turner confirmed that he had seen Lewis Jeremiah Avershaw discharge the pistols, receiving a wound himself from one, and the contents of the other wounding David Price, who died very shortly afterwards. The surgeon confirmed that Price's death was as a consequence of the wound.

Jerry looked at his counsel, Mr Knowles and Mr Best, who returned despondent grimaces. They knew that the weight of evidence against Jerry was too strong to be defended robustly.

Mr Baron Perryn summed up the evidence and addressed the jury with a final statement. 'The counsel for the prisoner has principally rested their defence on the fact that several other persons were present when the pistols were discharged. They claim that the death wound may well have been inflicted by someone else. However, the jury should remember that Officer Turner has sworn positively that he saw the prisoner in the act of discharging the contents of the pistols.'

The jury took only three minutes to decide upon a guilty verdict, but Mr Knowles and Mr Best weren't quite finished yet. They immediately placed an objection to the verdict on the grounds that Avershaw's indictment was flawed, as it didn't specifically state that David Price had died in St Saviours parish.

After a long argument, Mr Baron Perryn said that he would seek the opinion of the Twelve Judges of England, but the counsel for the prosecution then insisted that Jerry Avershaw be tried on the second indictment of feloniously shooting at Officer Barnaby Windsor, for which there was the support of a single witness. Consequently, Jerry was tried on the second indictment, and the verdict again came quickly – "the prisoner is found guilty".

During all of this, Jerry had acted with a great deal of restraint, much to everyone's surprise. The vultures that had descended upon the assizes to be entertained weren't about to be let down, though, as Jerry finally fixed his ice-cold intimidating glare upon Judge Baron Perryn. 'Am I to be murdered on the evidence of one witness?'

His question went unanswered. 'I said, am I to be murdered on the evidence of one fucking witness?' Jerry repeated. However, the court's deliberations had ended and there was no more to be said. Jerry's dreadful predicament had come to its conclusion.

There was a hint of theatre as Judge Baron Perryn reached for his judicial black cap, slowly and deliberately gathered it and methodically placed it upon his heavily powdered wig. It carried all the hallmarks of a self-proclaimed ceremony. It was his moment, that moment in time when all eyes were upon him, and him only; the moment he was keen to share between himself and his spellbound audience.

Jerry watched the judge. *This is what keeps the old bastard going*, he thought to himself before picking up his own hat and placing it on his head and setting about mimicking the judge's every move, mocking his deadpan expression and his slow measured movements. The public gallery tittered. This was what they had come to see. The hours of waiting and watching had been rewarded to them tenfold. The cocky arrogant highwayman gave them what they wanted.

Jerry's thoughts, however, weren't in keeping with that of his unworthy onlookers. He just wanted to scuttle the judge's sacred moment, which was all so dear to him, and steal his thunder with sneering looks, while cursing and ridiculing him and the jury as the death sentence was passed. *Why not? What are they going to do? Hang me twice?* he thought.

Newgate Prison, London
30 July 1795

'THE BLACK cherries you asked for,' said the turnkey as he handed Jerry a large bowl laden to excess.

'What do I owe you?' asked Jerry.

'Nothing. When the shopkeeper knew who they were for, he sent them with his compliments and great sadness. He said he remembered you from way back. Bill Sayers, his name is.'

Jerry gave a wry smile as he popped one of the cherries into his mouth, spitting the pip into a nearby bowl before reaching into his coat pocket to pay the turnkey for his favour.

'So kind, Jerry, so kind. Anything you need, just ask.' Jerry thought back to ten years or so earlier when he and Henry had been caught red-handed attempting to steal apples from the front of Bill Sayers's shop. The former pugilist grabbed Jerry by the scruff of the neck, while Henry managed to make his escape. Jerry inhaled deeply before expelling the air through his nostrils as he grinned to himself like an old man reminiscing of days gone by.

It all came back to him. The stern words barked from the stocky, bull-like shopkeeper: 'Don't you go nicking things, you ungovernable little bastard. If you're desperate for an apple, come and see me. You do a little job or errand for me and you get an apple, but don't fucking steal from me.' Jerry remembered washing the windows of Bill's shop for him that day, for that crisp shiny apple. He remembered how Bill polished the apple on his spotless apron before handing it to him. He also remembered that the windows had already sparkled like stars in the sky before setting about the task with his bucket of water and cloth. They didn't need washing, as they had already been cleaned earlier that morning. Bill Sayers just wanted to instil some work ethic into him and place him in a better mindset. It worked for a day, but that was about it.

Jerry sat down facing the wall in his cell like an artist contemplating a blank canvas. The black cherries that he'd commissioned were to be shared between himself and the dismal walls that incarcerated him, placing one every so often into his mouth while passing his time daubing child-like pictures with his fingers with the juice of the others.

The pictures were all of himself, alone, never accompanied, holding up coaches and post-chaises on the king's highway, pistol in hand, barking the words "damn your eyes, stop", with a few other expletives thrown in here and there for good measure. It was clear there was no remorse, no intention of attempting to repair all the wrongs he'd done in the final stages of his young life. It was yet another way of telling all who entered his cell that he lived the life of a high toby and when that moment came to be "turned off", he would die like a high toby, and there was nothing anyone could do about it.

'Someone to see you, Jerry,' said the turnkey, almost apologetically. The visitor pushed past the turnkey, his tall muscular frame overshadowing the small ageing jailer, making him look somewhat insignificant. The old turnkey nodded and smiled before locking the door behind him and taking his leave.

Jerry's eyes beamed in the bleak darkness of his cold, damp cell upon the sight of his friend Lance Andrews. Lance hugged his friend whilst looking around the small condemned cell, which had been transformed by Jerry's primitive art work. Lance kept his thoughts to himself. He always tried to place himself in the other person's shoes before giving his opinion about a situation and, given that Jerry's predicament was as bleak as it gets, he more than understood where he was coming from. *Do whatever helps you through this, my friend*, Lance thought to himself, knowing this was to be the end of the road for their long, close, friendship.

Newgate Prison
2 August 1795, Midnight

JERRY LAY back in his cell, hands tucked firmly behind his head, legs crossed. The condemned highwayman counted the hours of his remaining existence. Twenty-two years of age, soon to be twenty-three, a high toby from the tender age of seventeen. Everything he'd done in his life had been done earlier than it should have been. The short transformation from boy to man had materialised far too quickly. Maybe it was inevitable that his fateful end would be no different.

His deep thoughts were suddenly intruded upon by the thunderous clanging of a large hand bell along the corridor from his cell. He knew exactly what this was. He'd been expecting its appearance, but it still caught him off his guard. Clang! Clang! Clang!

All you that in the condemned hole do lie,
Prepare you, for tomorrow you shall die.
Watch all, and pray, the hour is drawing near,
That you before Almighty God must appear.
Examine well yourselves, in time repent,
That you not to eternal flames be sent,
And when St Sepulchre's bell tomorrow tolls,
The Lord above, have mercy on your souls.

The bell clanged twelve times on the midnight hour. The well-known death knell was obligatory to all condemned on their last night on this earth.

Kennington Common, London
3 August 1795

THE CROWDS stretched shoulder to shoulder along Kennington Common, further than the eye could see. Some were quiet, respectful, even subdued, keeping their innermost thoughts to themselves. Others, however, were of a completely different disposition. Their love affair with the gin bottle seemed by far the strongest bond they had with anything in their dishevelled dismal lives. Their crass laughter and gutter rat behaviour made for a moment in Gin Lane rather than an execution.

The printers' work was now complete, as they handed out their fresh-off-the-press broadsheets for the princely sum of one penny to eager outstretched hands, desperate to find out more about the appalling villainous atrocities of the living nightmare that stalked their highways and commons with a reign of terror akin to Satan himself. Many were about to see him for the first time in living flesh, and of course also for the last time. No opportunity was missed with such a vast congregation of enthusiastic people. It was a good opportunity to capitalise on the misfortune of somebody else.

At noon, back at Newgate Prison, preparations were underway to transport Jerry Avershaw to his final destination.

'On to the cart, backs to the horse's tail,' barked the hangman to the three condemned souls but the hangman's piercing eyes focused on those of Jerry, and his alone, as he searched for tell-tale signs of despondency, depression, anxiety and weakness, but none were to be found.

Jerry looked back at him, staring hard. The hangman blinked against his will and then nodded with respect. The outlaw was going to be in control to the bitter end and the hangman knew it. He'd seen it all before, and that short, intense split-second encounter told him all he needed to know – there was going to be nothing in the way of remorse. Jerry climbed uncaringly on to the cart.

He was to share his final moments with two other convicted souls bound on the same slow journey across London Bridge into his hometown and on to Kennington Common to meet with their undignified fate. The others looked highly unlikely candidates to share a cart with one of London's most notorious highwaymen.

Sarah King, a young brunette woman of slender stature, sat head bowed and petrified. She was to meet her unsavoury end for the murder of her illegitimate baby son. A hollow look of sadness and deep regret lay etched across her gaunt, pale face. Her moment of insanity was soon to be accounted for. The taking of the life of her son weighed heavily on her, and the life of her own in all probability would have been taken by her own hand also, rather than the hangman, had she been left to ponder over the consequences of her moment of uncontrollable madness.

The other was a quietly spoken religious man by the name of John Little, who resided in Kew and worked as a curator in the laboratory at Kew observatory in the Old Deer Park at Richmond. Little had become a favourite of the king and often attended walks through the observatory gardens with him and his small entourage, but unfortunately, as is sometimes the case with certain individuals of the human race, what you see isn't always what you get.

Little had borrowed money from a friend, a kind elderly gentleman by the name of William Macevoy, who lived in the lane adjoining Kew and Richmond. John Little was rather slow in coming forward to repay the old man's generosity, prompting Mr Macevoy to gently jolt his memory. It wasn't what the borrower wanted to hear, and he repaid the old man's kindness by climbing through the window of his home in the still of night and beating him to death with a large stone.

His actions hadn't gone unheard and he was disturbed in the middle of his barbaric act by William Macevoy's elderly housekeeper Sarah King, who ironically had the same name as the woman who was sharing his cart to the gallows. Little had turned his attention upon her, inflicting the exact same beating. Her cries for help had alerted the neighbours, who immediately ran to fetch the local constable, who happened to live nearby. Sarah had died of her hideous wounds.

John Little had not made his escape while he had the chance, instead deciding to hide himself in the large chimney of his victim's home, with the intention of sneaking off quietly when things had calmed. It was a grave miscalculation, for he was soon found and brought to justice.

John Little was also rumoured to have been involved in the unsolved murder of a man by the name of Arthur Stroud, whose body had been found lying under an iron vice in the octagon room of Kew observatory. But for all his fame of being acquainted with His Majesty and the infamy of the "Kew Murders" he wasn't the rogue that the public had flocked in their droves to see. The star attraction was the constable-killing outlaw who had spread fear all over the metropolis, Lewis Jeremiah Avershaw.

'Let the show begin.' Laughed the highwayman, as the heavily laden cart's wheels creaked into motion. The under-sheriff and prison chaplain led the procession, along with the hangman and his assistants. The cart was followed by a troop of javelin men on horseback.[4] Jerry didn't waste any time with his intrigued onlookers, venting his frustrated anger upon the stern-faced javelin men as they trotted slowly behind him. The crowd roared their approval at every sharp sarcastic quip that Jerry threw towards the javelin men.

When that point of no return and acceptance to the dreaded inevitable prevails, a whole new line of thought arises. Jerry had met with that scenario several days earlier. The crowd was clearly and somewhat strangely on his side, despite this being a man who, without a moment's hesitation, would have relieved them of all that was dear to them had they the misfortune to cross his path or dared to look at him longer than they should have in a tavern.

And despite such an event being likely to conclude in bad repercussions of one type or another, the crowd took it upon themselves and foolishly decided that maybe if they had met with Jerry under different circumstances, they might well have got along with the crude but amusing fellow. After all, he clearly showed ample courage and prowess, which was clearly a much-prized attribute to all attending. If you had a wicked sense of humour in your darkest hour and died gamely, that was more than enough to send them all back to their mundane little worlds feeling contented, to blabber on endlessly about yet another charismatic high toby who had impregnated himself into the history books of England's folklore.

The local heathens who regularly attended the hangings were in abundance, but noticeably subdued. Gone were the mindless acts of throwing the first heavy object that came to hand, whilst taunting the condemned with sadistic vigour as

---

[4] Guards

they made their way to the gallows. The regulars were more than aware that Henry Watts and the residue of Avershaw's gang were still at large and quite possibly concealed amongst the more protective elements of the crowd. Rumour had it that they were going to blatantly snatch their man before "the hemp brushed his neck" and make good their escape through a corridor of armed sympathisers in the crowd. It was certainly something that couldn't be dismissed or taken lightly.

Friends and acquaintances of the condemned followed alongside the cart like loyal hounds following their master.

It was a bizarre sight, and one would be forgiven for thinking they were paid bodyguards for the notorious highwayman in the event of last-minute liberty being aimed in his direction.

Meanwhile, Jerry Avershaw continued with his flippant show, waving to those who knew him, raising his eyebrows and pointing to them with a smile as they called back, 'Fuck 'em Jerry! Fuck 'em!'

Clouds of disturbed dust floated up into the air from the horse's hooves, as the summer heat intensified, adding to the javelin men's discomfort.

'If I'm going to be twisted, what better a day for it.' Laughed Jerry to the crowd, hands raised towards the blistering sun, like some messiah about to address his followers. However, the comparison ended there. His waistcoat and shirt were by now unbuttoned to the waist, exposing his chest in true high toby style, and he had a sprig of myrtle clenched between his teeth. His fellow sufferers hadn't been given a second thought. They had by now become virtually invisible to all in attendance.

The strong overpowering personality of the highwayman was even more prominent as the cart slowed to a grinding halt on the south side of the bridge. He was now in the parish that had watched him grow from child to man. The crowd had spilled into their path as a fight broke out between two young women. Jerry looked around, taking in as much as he possibly could, his eyes catching sight of a careworn figure selling meat pies to the crowd, taking full advantage of the many well-lined pockets in attendance.

Jerry recognised her instantly – it was "Juicy" Joyce Cotton, Wolf Winterman's aunt, whose nickname had supposedly originated from the selling of her juicy oranges. However, those in the know knew that the nickname came from her rather more unsavoury side-line of the past, entertaining many of her more visually attractive young male customers with her charms, albeit for a small fee of course. She was always on the lookout to make as much money by the easiest means possible, her work ethic bordering on the lethargic side to say the least. Wolf used to say that the only time she would get out of her gin-soaked bed early would be the day the house was on fire.

Juicy Joyce looked at Jerry with an irritated, contemptuous smirk, whilst giving him a "so what" shrug of her bony shoulders. There was no love lost between them. They had never cared for each other much, but this was the first time it had clearly become apparent. *A penny before everything*, Jerry thought to himself as his derisory gaze swept over her.

He recollected the first time he'd set eyes on her, standing beside her orange barrow smoking a clay pipe. The passing years hadn't been kind to her, no matter what way you looked at it. The perimeter of her mouth was heavily pitted with those deep incisions normally to be found on a person of far more advanced years. The majority of her teeth had long since parted company with her mouth, and the corners of her eyes carried the compulsory crow's feet that come from a forever squinting smoker.

Jerry remembered how Wolf grumbled incessantly about her and how she exploited his Uncle Jimmy from the very first moment they began courting, never having a good word to say about any of his close friends that he'd grown up with from knee high. At any God-given opportunity she'd get the knives out and set about stabbing them in the back, systematically setting about driving them away until his old friends became non-existent. She then gently introduced her new-found drinking cronies into their little world, dropping them in one at a time until Jimmy was surrounded by her choice of friends only.

Wolf's uncle was a good-hearted man, but unfortunately not the sharpest tool in the box. He was too busy working all the hours he could get his hands on at the Port of London down by Billingsgate to notice Joyce's conniving ways. The process took shape slowly over time, but Wolf knew all too well how Joyce could manipulate a situation to her own advantage. In his world, the likes of Juicy Joyce Cotton were ten a penny and that's why he kept her at arm's length. 'Keep smiling. Keep smiling,' the harsh, somewhat croaky voice of a man rang out above all others in the crowd. 'You won't be smiling soon when they sling your lifeless body on to the death cart, ha ha.' Spluttered the intoxicated wretch who stood in the company of Juicy Joyce Cotton.

'Looking at the state of you, you won't make it to find out.' Retaliated one of the hounds running alongside the cart as he unleashed a heavy blow to the side of the man's head, sending him sprawling to the ground. The crowd roared. Jerry laughed with them, while John Little and Sarah King looked on despondently.

The cart continued on its morbid carnival-like procession. As it reached Kennington Common the full magnitude of the disturbing occasion became apparent. The larger than usual crowds that peppered the narrow streets should have been a warning of what lay ahead, but nothing could have prepared them for the sight that unfolded before their eyes. The crowd was huge, far beyond anyone's comprehension, the noise deafening. John Little and Sarah King looked as if they had drifted into a state of mental meltdown. The feral crowd's wails and chants and the mere sight of the gallows' timbers cutting into the skyline disconnected something inside them. Their worst nightmare was about to unfold before their very eyes, and there was nothing they could do about it.

The cart's journey had come to its end, its wheels stopping beneath the gallows with inch-perfect precision. The under-sheriff and prison chaplain were the first to approach the rear of the cart, while the accused sat below their nooses, and the hangman and his accomplices stood close by. A young, tear-filled unknown woman in the crowd threw a sprig of myrtle to the condemned highwayman, much to the annoyance of John Townsend, who was in attendance. The woman's looks reminded him far too much of Rosie. It brought him grave discomfort.

The newsmen standing close by effected horror that the outlaw was continuing to the very last moment of his existence in the same hardened state, making them re-evaluate their thoughts on the human race, as he ignored his fellow sufferers beside him.

Jerry cursed every word the clergyman endeavoured to say to him, throwing the obligatory bible, that was handed to all condemned in the hope that they would repent at the last minute and go to a better place, into the crowd with vindictive contempt. He was also cursing John Townsend and the under-sheriff with implications of their poor performance with their wives in their private moments. He then proceeded to kick off his boots, telling the crowd that he wished to prove his mother wrong and that he wouldn't die with his boots on.

When the executioner took the whip and touched the horse's tail, Jerry made a spring from the cart, and was heard to repeat the curse that had put fear into all that crossed his path: 'Damn your fucking eyes!' These were the last words that the notorious highwayman ever spoke.

His two fellow sufferers died slowly from the "short drop" beside him – three different people, three different personalities, one common bond, murder. The neither here nor there attitude of the crowd as John Little and Sarah King took their exit from the world may well have been the way the two would have preferred their executions to pan out, their suffering and humiliation overshadowed and somewhat unnoticed as the crowd lavished their attention on the notorious outlaw. It's not for everyone, the limelight. People aren't the same, either in life or in death.

Later in the day, the streets of London were silent and still; nobody was there. It was an unusual, somewhat eerie sight. A lone dog wandered down the road, and as it passed an open window it became momentarily startled by the sudden hail of abuse resonating from a disenchanted mother, ticking off her child. The dog looked back at the window as it skedaddled away, tail between its legs, as if the reprimanding words were directed at itself. On a normal, busy, bustling day this probably wouldn't have had the same sharp impact, but the day's unusual tranquillity seemed to magnify everything out of all proportion.

You could occasionally hear the humble sparrows chirping from the rooftops, but the usual clip, clop, clip, clop of horses' hooves and rumble of cart wheels were noticeably absent. It seemed as if everyone from miles around had made their way over to Putney Bottom to view the lifeless body of Lewis Jeremiah Avershaw as he hung in his gibbet cage, guarded by mounted soldiers and police on the orders of John Townsend and the military. No more embarrassing moments were going to materialise from opportunistic members of Avershaw's gang. Any visions of stealing their friend's body away would be unduly crushed. In fact, John Townsend's thoughts had been correct, as visits had indeed been made, and ideas duly dissolved, although not abandoned. Eyes were watching and waiting for the first signs of egotistical entanglement between the two guarding factions in the hope of creating a favourable opportunity. Just one small hiccup was all that was needed, and besides, how long could this vigil over their friend continue? After all, time is money, and the Runners would need to return to far more pressing concerns, as would the military with the ever-problematic French. The outlaws were certain that the waiting game would be short-lived.

After all, time was very much on their side.

The Sword Blade Coffee House, Birching Lane
22 August 1795, 10.30 am

'DID YOU know, Dick, how it came about…the burying of our plunder after a little bit of villainy, and then returning to it at a safer point in time?' Henry Watts asked Dick Ferguson.

'No, Henry,' replied Dick, 'but to hazard a guess I'd say you picked it up from George.'

'No, no. Although you could be forgiven for thinking that of course. After all, he did teach us so much over the years. No, it was a brainstorm of our Jerry's. We first started doing it at the age of fourteen, after sitting on the edge of Kennington Common one morning, not too far from a water trough for the sheep and cattle. We watched a magpie as it hopped on to the trough without giving our presence a second thought, then it scooped up some water, quenching its thirst. We were fascinated at the way it tilted it's head in the air as it drank. It looked to us like it was gargling. Jerry started mimicking it, gargling noises and all. It was an amusing thing to see,' Henry said with a reminiscing smile, as if he were back in the moment.

'It was a hot summer's day in the middle of June if I remember correctly,' continued Henry. 'That magpie hopped down on to the ground and picked up a piece of stale bread that had been left behind by some of the farm hands who had been repairing the fences. It then returned back to the trough, dipping the bread in to soften it before devouring it. It repeated this a few times before taking the rest a short distance away to feed its young, which were perched like soldiers in a row on a fence nearby.

'The following day we returned to the very same spot, around much the same time, waiting to meet some mates, when our little black-and-white friend made its appearance once again. There was no bread left behind by the farmers this time, but we noticed it had bread in its beak. It hopped back on to the trough and dipped it into the water again and replicated its procedure from the day before by feeding its young on the same bit of fence nearby. It then went away for a moment and returned with more bread and repeated the process.

'Jerry looked at me all bright-eyed and said, "That bird has taken all the bread that was here yesterday and stored it somewhere else so no other birds can get it, then returned for it at a later point in time when needed. That's what we should do with our plunder after we've robbed a property, reducing the risk of being apprehended on the day of the theft."'

'We did just that from that day on and it worked. All down to that magpie. The things you can learn from nature eh,' Henry said with a sober smile.

'Initiative, Henry, that's what that is. Looking through the woods and not seeing only the trees,' said Dick, acknowledging his friend's trip down memory lane.

Henry rubbed at the back of his tense neck. 'For sure, my friend, for sure.'

The Bald-Faced Stag Inn, Putney Vale
Later That Day

HENRY WALKED over to a chest of drawers that sat in the corner of the room, sliding the top drawer open and removing a small bone-handled knife. The blade had been ground down, rendering it to half its original thickness. He gently laid it on top of the sill of the window, before proceeding to place his hands behind the heavy chest, prising it away from the wall until it exposed the floorboards beneath.

He dropped to his knees and ran the blade of his knife between the narrow cavity of the boards. Billy watched with fascination as Henry retrieved a dusty hemp cord, pulling it gently towards himself, releasing a hidden spring, forcing the board to jump up like a jack-in-the-box.

'Genius, Henry, bloody genius,' whispered Billy as he watched eagerly, anticipating what his friend was about to retrieve. As the objects came into view, Billy gulped heavily. 'Are they what I think they are Henry?' he asked.

'I don't know. What are you thinking?' asked Henry calmly.

'Are they Jerry's pistols from the Three Brewers?'

'Aye, that they are. These are the little beauties we liberated from the three captains. Bocka Drey was drinking with Jerry at the time and had the presence of mind to grab the guns and have it on his toes out the back door during all the mayhem. He then brought them to me. He thought they might not have a case if the guns weren't around, but that didn't work, did it? It didn't hinder the trial at all, so here they are, just waiting to embarrass the military a little more.'

Henry pointed to the secret compartment, adding, 'I had the third pistol stored down there all the time. Now all three are back in my possession.' He walked back over to the window and inhaled deeply before walking over to his coat that was sprawled on a chair. He reached into his coat pocket and removed his watch, looking at it despondently. 'Where the hell are Dick and James? Their timekeeping is worse than yours, and that's saying something.'

Billy looked at him, blushing slightly, then shrugging his shoulders gingerly. 'Who knows?' he replied. 'Maybe they've been held up by scamps. I hear it's not safe around this neck of the woods even at this time of the day.'

Henry looked hard at Billy, his stony face breaking into a reluctant smile as the sound of horses outside cut short his friend's prattle. Henry returned to the window, but it was only a pair of tinkers passing by. 'Where the hell are they?' he asked worriedly. Henry was showing unusual signs of restlessness and agitation.

Just a few moments earlier, as Dick and James had approached the Bald Faced Stag, they had realised that something was wrong. Jack the landlord and old Ralph the ostler were standing at the front door of the inn talking to two Bow Street Runners. Dick and James turned their horses sharply into a nearby spinney and dismounted, watching apprehensively to see what was about to unfold. It didn't look good at all.

'I hope and pray that Henry and Billy tired of waiting for us and didn't stay around,' said Dick miserably, as he watched the men talking outside the inn.

'I didn't realise you were a religious man, Dick,' teased James half-heartedly, as he watched beside him.

'I bloody ain't but if there's half a chance of some bearded fellow sitting up there watching down on us, we could do with a hand right now.'

Their moment of despair turned to a sense of helplessness and uncontrollable anguish as the grim realisation of their worst imaginings unfolded in front of them. A further six soldiers and Runners turned into view from the side of the inn, exiting from the stables. In their custody were Henry and Billy, mounted on their horses, legs chained beneath their horses' bellies.

'Oh no. Where did they get those from?' said Dick, as they watched John Townsend hand over three pistols to a captain for scrutiny. The captain nodded and they were handed back, placed into a bag and taken away along with Henry and Billy.

James and Dick left their horses in the safe seclusion of the spinney and cautiously made their way to the inn's stable door.

'You shouldn't be around here, lads,' said old Ralph with deep concern. 'This is as serious as it gets. I don't know if this has anything to do with you boys, but if it does, you'd better give your situation some considerable thought.'

'What makes you think it has anything to do with us, Ralph?' asked Dick inquisitively.

'If it didn't, you'd have turned up on your horses, boys, instead of leaving them down the road in the spinney.'

'How do you know where we left our horses?' asked James, as he watched the old man stuff tobacco into a pipe that had seen better days. Both men noticed he was shaking uncontrollably. The incident had shaken him badly.

'One and one makes two, boys. One and one makes two,' Ralph replied. 'I think you should both come with me and have a word with Jack.' The ageing ostler marched through the door like a man half his age, calling abruptly to the landlord, 'Jack! I think you should take the lads up to Henry's room and let them see for themselves what the uniforms found.'

Jack removed his apron and cast it on to the bar. 'Come with me,' he instructed, 'and lets be quick about it. You boys sure as hell can't stay around here for too long. This lot aren't in the mood to forgive and forget.'

The men made their way up the stairs and entered Henry's room. Their eyes were instantly drawn to the displaced chest of drawers that had exposed the dismantled floorboard.

'Henry had the guns in there boys,' said Jack. 'They were caught red-handed. I didn't have a chance to warn them. Townsend's and that captain's moves were calculated and so bloody fast that nothing was left to chance. They asked me many questions but received no worthwhile answers. I told them that Henry and others took rooms here for short periods from time to time as they were often on the move because they were horse and cattle dealers. That's what Jerry had told me to tell any over-inquisitive busybodies.

'Oh, and Townsend asked if they always used the same rooms each time they visited. I told them no. I knew that was what they didn't want to hear. Townsend then asked what I knew of the floorboard mechanism, but before I had a chance to answer, that snooty captain interrupted and said sarcastically, "Don't tell me, let me guess, you know nothing of this either, even though it's on your own fucking property." That pair of bastards looked at me and Ralph with pure contempt, I can tell you. I wouldn't be surprised if it isn't the last we see of them, but the truth of the matter is I didn't know a thing about Henry's handiwork, and that captain wouldn't stop squawking about the fact that the three men who robbed him and his fellow captains had now been taken out of the public domain for the better of everybody.'

Dick cast a look of horror towards James before returning his full attention back to Jack, saying, 'Billy wasn't there Jack. I'm not saying who was, but it wasn't him. He's being accused of something he didn't do.'

'Well, unless the perpetrator of the crime goes running into Bow Street Station waving his hands in the air and shouting at the top of his voice. "It wasn't Billy who did it, it was me, guv." The future doesn't look too bloody healthy for him does it? And the chances of that happening, someone confessing to a certain death penalty when they can sit back and let someone else take the blame for it…well, it goes without saying, doesn't it lads.'

'That person will just have to live out the rest of his days with that young man's death set firmly at the forefront of his mind. Every morning when he rises to a bright new day, he'll remember that a wrongly condemned young man should be doing just that instead of himself. It's a dilemma I sure as hell wouldn't want to have hanging over my head. Battling day in and day out with the authorities is one thing but battling day in and day out with your own conscience is another thing altogether.'

James Myers looked at Dick, intrigued at how he was going to respond, but the moment passed without a reply. The two highwaymen sat for a while and pondered over their next move before returning to the spinney, only to find their horses fitted with nosebags, feeding merrily in the care of old Ralph.

'Always thinking, Ralph. What would we do without you?' said James before they slid away unnoticed into the green expanse of the common.

'You know something, Dick?' said James as they rode. 'That captain must feel eighteen hands high, capturing Henry and Billy and regaining possession of those pistols. When you think about it, what were the chances of him seeing them ever again? I for one wouldn't have placed good money against such odds. That's the kind of thing that would rest well with man and woman alike. Everybody would want to recuperate what they once lost if that thing is dear to them.'

James looked over at Dick, who clearly wasn't engaged with the conversation. 'What's running through that mind of yours my friend?' he asked. 'I can clearly see the wheels going around.'

'I was thinking that even when Billy tells them he wasn't there, nobody's going to listen. They must all feel they have closure, and when that's installed so adamantly, who on earth is going to want to listen? It's going to be job done, mission accomplished, let's raise the anchor and sail off into the sunset.'

'But don't beat yourself up over it, Dick. If Billy was in your shoes, he'd be doing the self-same thing, no different to anyone else. It's alright to talk like a hero, but to walk through Townsend's door knowing you're surrendering to instant death…well, the survival instinct kicks in doesn't it. If it was your little brother or sister, that's a different story, but it isn't.'

Dick looked at his friend, whose words were failing miserably in giving him any solace. It had become apparent that Dick's battle with his inner being had already begun. Henry Watts's powers had been weakened considerably with the loss of his childhood friend Jerry, and now with his own incarceration, his reputation fell into the category of yesterday's worries. Things had begun to take on a whole new dimension. Their little closed shop was beginning to feel as if the back door had been left wide open.

The people that James and Dick had previously trusted without giving a second thought were now viewed through cynical eyes. They became aware that certain elements didn't carry the same feelings of loyalty and respect that were so abundantly bestowed upon their friends. Trust was indeed becoming a far more fragile commodity than they would have wished. It was going to take time to rebuild certain bridges and reinforce trust amongst those that believed they were too risky to do business with.

'I think I know why Henry wanted to speak to us today, Dick,' said James.

'Do tell me, James, I'm all ears,' replied Dick.

'I think he was going to talk to us about retrieving Jerry's body.'

'Well, if that was the case, James, I'd say it's no longer a matter that should hold any consideration at this moment in time because circumstances have changed. It's more than clear that these pit bulls bite, and bite fucking hard, without letting go. Jerry's dead and surrounded by guards around the clock. They're determined to make an example of him and anyone who has any ideas about liberating his body. These people would be more than pleased to eliminate the lot of us from the face of the earth.'

'That's a valid point, a very valid point,' agreed James. 'You're right, sometimes in life you must let things go. Maybe when the authorities realise that we're not going to make any efforts to steal him away they'll call it a day. After all, time is money is it not? Sooner or later some bigwig is going to say enough is enough, and then we can go get him and give him his burial.

'In the meantime, I think we should make ourselves scarce so we can clear our minds and give ourselves some quality thinking time, and I think I know just the place. My cousin has a small farm in Purfleet, Essex. Nothing fancy, but out of the way.'

'Purfleet you say. I've never been to Purfleet,' said Dick.

'Well, it sits on the river about sixteen miles east on the other side of the bridge and, like I said, it's out of the way, although his nearest neighbour is the Purfleet gunpowder magazine, with a garrison, obviously, to protect it.'

'Obviously,' said Dick, looking closely at his friend with a look of uncertainty, wondering whether he'd just lost his mind.

'No, seriously, Dick. Think about it for a moment. If you're going to lay low, why not right under the military's noses. Of course, a change of clothes will be needed, but my cousin will take care of that.'

'Are you sure he won't mind having us around?' asked Dick.

'Aye, I'm sure,' James assured him. 'If anything, he'll be over the moon, glad of the company.'

'Good, James. That sounds like a plan, but before we make tracks, there's something I must do.'

Police Office, Union Hall, London, 23 August 1795

'THERE'S A young boy outside, guv, with a letter. He wishes to hand it to you personally or not at all. He tells me it's of much importance to you,' Corporal Boare informed John Townsend, who was sitting in his office.

'Oh my, the drama of it all. Bring him in,' instructed Townsend.

Corporal Boare turned on his heels and walked briskly to the open door. 'Young man!' he called abruptly, before beckoning him over with a wave of his hand. 'You're in luck. Mr Townsend will give you a minute of his time, so be sharp.' The young boy marched over to the threshold of the door and waited for a signal to enter.

'Come in, come in, young man,' Townsend said, as Corporal Boare led the boy in. 'I've been informed by my corporal that you have a letter of some importance. It must be terribly important that it not be trusted with anybody but little old me, don't you think?'

'Yes, sir. I've been given strict orders that it's to reach your possession and your possession only.'

'Well, indeed it has, so well done, you.' The young boy smiled, pleased with his accomplishment.

'My, it has a wax seal and all,' said Townsend. 'This letter must be very, very important, don't you think, Corporal?'

'Oh yes, guv, anything with a seal must be of exceptional importance,' replied the corporal, playing along with the classroom banter. He watched as Townsend opened the letter carefully and slowly in order to conceal his overwhelming curiosity, before running his eyes over it with an amused grin. His amusement was short-lived as he continued to read further, however.

Corporal Boare winced as he looked on, watching John Townsend's demeanour take on a far more serious mantle.

The letter read as follows:

Mr Townsend,

I write to you with the good knowledge that you're a man of boundless logic and fair play. If I didn't believe these qualities were held within you, I wouldn't have wasted my time with this letter.

You have under your lock and key two of my good friends, with the inaccurate belief that they're the men who plundered three captains on Wimbledon Common, taking amongst other things their military pistols. I've also been informed that Henry Watts's horse was identified without question by one of the captains outside the stables of the Bald Faced Stag on the day of their apprehension, and later reinforced by the other captains.

The question I ask you, sir, is this: why did they fail to recognise Bill's horse? The answer to this is as clear as a fine summer's day to me, so I think I should share it with you. Billy Frampton was not there on that evening. I know this because it wasn't him but myself who was there that evening. He's without question an innocent man who was in the wrong place at the wrong time. I'm sure he's already told you this, and that he was unaware of what he was about to be shown as you moved in to apprehend them.

Your capture of Henry with the guns must have looked like a well-timed open and shut case for you but I'm afraid to say that this is far from the truth, giving you a misleading conclusion. If it isn't too much to ask, please take yourself to your window, then you'll see the man and horse you're looking for.

Not yours until
captured, Richard (Dick)
Ferguson.

John Townsend handed the letter to his corporal, who calmly read through it without the slightest inkling of an expression.

'A look out of the window is far too good an opportunity to be ignored, don't you think, Corporal?' suggested Townsend.

Corporal Boare agreed. 'Far too good an opportunity, guv. Let's go take a look. My curiosity is beginning to get the better of me.'

The two policemen peered out of the window, scrutinising every male that came into view. The thought of being hoaxed began to play on their minds as they glanced at one another with perplexed looks. They needn't have concerned themselves because moments later an immaculately dressed man mounted on a fine chestnut gelding trotted arrogantly into view, cockily removing his top hat and greeting his pursuers with a wave more akin to the king himself, before whipping his horse into a gallop down the street and around the corner out of sight.

'The nerve of that cocky bastard,' growled Corporal Boare, unable to keep his emotions to himself.

John Townsend turned his attention back to the young boy. 'How long have you known this man?' he asked.

'Only since this morning, sir,' the boy replied.

'Just since this morning?' enquired Townsend with suspicion.

'Yes, sir,' confirmed the boy.

'And how much did he pay you for bringing this letter to me?' asked Townsend.

'One shilling, sir.'

'Did he give you a reason why he asked you to deliver the letter instead of doing it himself?'

'Yes, sir, he told me you wrongly arrested his friend, and that it was he and not the other man who should have been arrested. He said the letter would explain his friend's innocence.'

John Townsend looked into the boy's eyes, saying, 'Well, thank you, young man, for your help. Corporal Boare, would you kindly escort this young man off the premises.' The corporal didn't need to be asked twice, leading the boy away at speed, before returning to the office.

John Townsend shook his head in dismay and Corporal Boare tutted and also shook his head. 'I know I constantly keep saying it, Corporal,' said Townsend, 'but I never cease to be amazed by the antics of our fellow creatures. Never.'

'I know, guv, and that little creature we've just sent away is a type I've seen so many times before. It's that dead behind the eyes look that gives them away, and you can bet as sure as four farthings make a penny, that wasn't the first time he'd met with Ferguson.'

'I share your thoughts entirely, Corporal. He wasn't the l, twee little boy he was trying to make himself out to be. Very streetwise that one, for sure. I've a feeling that sometime in the future our paths will regrettably cross again.'

'Little acorns, heh, guv,' said Corporal Boare.

'Indeed, Corporal, little rotting acorns.' Agreed Townsend.

White's Gentlemen's Club, St James's Street, London 25 August 1795, 7.30 pm

'SO GLAD you could make it, Captain Hall,' said John Townsend with a sincere smile that was almost as large as the brandy he had cupped in his hand. 'And how are you, Captain Peregrine? Are we without the company of Captain Holt this evening?'

'Unfortunately, he has other pressing commitments, but sends his highest regards, along with his humblest apologies,' replied Captain Peregrine.

'Oh well, two's a close three I suppose. What are your tipples?' Townsend asked the two military officers.

'A brandy for me,' said Captain Peregrine enthusiastically, grasping the opportunity of his return by carriage to have one or maybe two more than he really should.

'Yes, I think I will have the same, thank you,' said Captain Hall. Townsend ordered the drinks from a passing waiter.

'I believe you have some information that may be of significant interest to us, Mr Townsend?' asked Captain Peregrine, momentarily casting aside all niceties and letting good old-fashioned curiosity get the better of his manners. 'Oh yes, indeed I do,' replied Townsend. 'Please forgive me, such thoughtlessness, me keeping you on tenterhooks.

You obviously want to know what's going on before relaxing and enjoying the rest of the evening, so I'll cut to the chase and enlighten you both.

'The day before yesterday I received a letter delivered to my office by a young boy. The letter was from someone by the name of Richard Ferguson, claiming that one of the men we had in custody for the dreadful liberty taken against yourselves wasn't there on that deplorable evening.'

John Townsend reached into the inside pocket of his coat with his free hand, retrieving a letter and handing it to Captain Hall, who read it with intensity and great speed before handing it to Captain Peregrine, who did likewise.

'How do you know this is not a deceitful ploy to free this Billy Frampton creature and then this Richard Ferguson could resort to complete denial of ever setting eyes on this document, rendering it useless?' suggested Captain Peregrine.

'Well, Captain Peregrine, I've read through this letter, not once, not twice, but several times, and I've repeatedly asked myself the very same question as that of Richard Ferguson. Why was Billy Frampton's horse not recognised in the same way as that of Henry Watts? After all, there were three of you there on that night. It seems to me that the only link we have with Billy Frampton is that of him being discovered at the lodgings of Henry Watts, who had in his possession your pistols.

'That, I'm afraid to say, isn't enough for a court of law to condemn a man for highway robbery, and the letter from Richard Ferguson confessing that it was he just adds weight to the fact that this young man wasn't there that evening.

'Please try to understand that I can only function on solid evidence. Past uneventful convictions due to making mistakes much like the one in front of us has taught me this the hard way.

'Trust me, Billy Frampton will be punished somewhere along the line, for he's certainly no angel, but not for the doings of Richard Ferguson. This is the man who robbed you alongside Watts and quite possibly Avershaw, and I'm quite sure that after your good selves give it the same amount of time and consideration you'll think likewise.'

Townsend began to feel unease and discomfort from Captain Hall's body language and narrowing of his eyes. 'Is there something bothering you, Captain Hall?' he asked with a hint of trepidation.

'Your expression, sir, when you talk of this Ferguson fellow disturbs me somewhat,' replied Captain Hall. 'I am under no illusion as to which side of the fence you sit as far as law and order is concerned, but your usual venom-spitting ways have become noticeably subdued when this man's name comes into the conversation.'

'Well, sometimes things aren't always black and white, Captain,' Townsend explained. 'As you being a man of the military will be well aware, you don't have to care for a certain individual to accept they have a quality within them that rings a bell in the room of respect. We all know talk is cheap, and this city of ours has more than its share of cheap talkers. Actions speak louder than words, don't you agree? 'I ask you this question,' continued Townsend. 'How many people do you know that if they really dug deep into their inner being would do what Richard Ferguson has done? As I say gentlemen, talk is cheap. Think hard and think deeply, place yourselves for a moment in this young man's shoes and understand the serious consequences he's levelled at himself. A very high percentage of people, when push comes to shove, would with all certainty sit back and make the decision to save their own skin. This man's decision, from all my worldly experiences, falls into the minority.'

'Quite possibly, sir, quite possibly,' replied Captain Hall. 'I will air your thoughts as I watch him swinging from the gallows.'

Purfleet, Essex, England
27 August 1795

DICK FERGUSON inhaled the cool morning air as he trotted his horse slowly down the narrow spiralling country lane. He'd just caught a view of the small ramshackle farmhouse that was to be his refuge for a short while. His initial grimace of displeasure mutated into a satisfying smile as he trotted his horse closer and closer.

He recognised a quaintness about the old house that rekindled fond memories of an old semi-derelict property he once played around as a child. It had the same feel of isolation and tranquillity, and it even had its own skylark that sang its heart out as it climbed higher and higher into the clear blue summer sky until finally disappearing from view.

'Well, what do you think?' asked James, tearing Dick away from his moment of reflection.

'The ultimate hideaway without question,' replied Dick, as his eyes steered back and forth, monitoring the house and half anticipating someone to make a welcoming appearance. But none was forthcoming.

They dismounted at the stables across from the house and made their way past the clucking bantams. They entered through the open kitchen door, where they found a dishevelled looking man straightening himself. He had a pair of bellows in hand and was standing next to a freshly lit fire that crackled and sparked as it built up momentum.

'I caught view of the pair of you as you made your way down the lane, so I thought I'd get a nice fire started, seeing there's a chill in the air,' the man said.

James squinted, then smiled as he crossed the kitchen floor to give his cousin a bear hug. 'This is my cousin, Olly.' He informed Dick. 'Olly, this is my trusted friend Dick Ferguson.'

'Nice to meet you, Dick, welcome to Owl Farm. I hope you enjoy your stay,' said Olly.

******

A week after arriving in Purfleet, Dick was peering out across the farmyard when an unaccompanied raindrop bounced off the window, drawing his attention up towards the grey threatening clouds that rolled slowly overhead.

'Do you ever get lonely out here in the back of beyond, without anyone to talk to, Olly?' Dick asked.

'Of course, I do. I'm not a crazy bloody recluse, you know,' Olly replied.

James looked at Olly, scratching his nose, with a wry grin on his face. 'Well, maybe not a recluse anyway,' he remarked, before reaching for another bottle of ale and topping up his tankard.

'Do you know something about Olly that I don't?' queried Dick, as he turned his back on the gloom of the day's weather and placed himself beside the far more appealing glow of the fire.

'We all have the odd skeleton tucked away in our cupboard,' Olly interjected, 'and I'm pretty damned sure that you two scoundrels are no different to an uninteresting farmer boy like me. We all have the odd naughty to live with.'

Dick looked at Olly with regenerated interest, asking, 'What makes you think I'm a scoundrel?'

Olly pointed towards James, ale bottle in hand. 'You're with him, aren't you? And you're hiding out here, are you not?'

Dick smiled in defeat and shrugged his shoulders. 'Do you have any family around this neck of the woods, Olly?' he asked.

'No, no. No family down here. The better side of our family died out some time ago, isn't that right, James?' James nodded in agreement. 'And the other side is sailing along merrily in Bermondsey, breeding like bloody rabbits. The sad thing is you can only cull the rabbits. If they're not fighting, stealing and breeding with strangers, they're doing it amongst themselves. The inbreeding must be something awful. There must be so many webbed hands and feet around there, I tell you.

'Best for me to be as far away from that lot as possible, that's what I say. Don't get me wrong, Dick, I'm not saying James and me are angels. No, no, far from it, but that shower has an irritating pettiness about them and no capacity to think beyond that of a scavenging rodent. To me, that's intolerable. Anybody with the slightest inkling of accountability in their souls would struggle to comprehend their tunnelled logic. They're beyond reason.

'You could call them out on some petty wrong they had done, and even though they were fully aware of their dirty deed, they would look you straight in the eye and give you some ridiculous utterings, void of all truth and substance, and stand by it no matter what. You can only take so much of that shit on a daily basis before you say enough is enough and head for the hills, leaving them to wallow in their homemade sewer.'

'It's nice to get things off your chest once in a while Olly. Have you missed anything?' said James with a giggle. 'No, I think I've just about covered everything. Forgive me, this is what happens when you're on your own for longer than you should be, with nobody to share your thoughts. You bottle things up and let it all out in one fell swoop at the first given opportunity.'

'Nothing wrong with that, Olly, we all have things we need to get off our chest from time to time,' said Dick, as he momentarily pondered over his next question, before plunging in with both feet. 'I hope you don't mind me asking Olly, but who was here with you before you ended up alone?'

'Huh, believe it or not, I was married, but things took a turn for the worse,' replied Olly.

'Turn for the worse?' asked Dick over-inquisitively.

James let out a frustrating sigh. 'Well, it was more like a shove over the cliff than a turn for the worse, wasn't it Olly?' he suggested. Olly shrugged his shoulders and curled his lip with a what's done is done attitude. 'Is it alright to tell him, Olly?' asked James, unsure how his cousin was going to respond to such serious questioning.

'Only if I can come on your next robbery,' suggested Olly. 'I need the money.'

'How good are you on a horse?' asked Dick. 'Faster than Satan riding the wind,' came the reply.

'Well, let James tell me your story, and if it's worth hearing, then maybe,' said Dick.

James looked at his cousin for approval and received the nod they wanted to see before commencing. 'As you know, Dick, farmers are often at the market,' said James, 'and Olly was no exception. If he wasn't selling, he was buying.

Well, it came to Olly's attention after one particular trip that some wretch from the garrison was taking it upon himself to nip around here and sample the goods that weren't for sale. The cheeky bastard used to ride down the lane as bold as brass and tether his horse outside the front door. His stupidity was beyond words, especially being a soldier and all. I suppose his regular little visits without being caught made him complacent. You know, familiarity breeds contempt, that sort of thing.'

Dick looked at the two men wide-eyed, asking, 'How did it all unfold?'

'Well, as I told you,' James continued, 'he would tether his horse outside the front door and Olly noticed the hoof marks. He didn't utter a word. It was early days to confront her about it. She would have probably just given him a pre-planned excuse anyway. So, as the next market day approached, he informed her that he'd be away a little longer than usual because the auction would be running late.

'As he told her this, he noticed her rubbing her clammy little hands on her apron as she flitted around the kitchen in a tizzy, right here where we're sitting as a matter of fact, trying her damnedest to conceal her inner excitement at being given more time to continue her nonsense with soldier boy.

'Well, unbeknown to her, after Olly left the house to go to market, he'd already planned to lay in wait a short distance up the lane. It wasn't long before he heard the clip clop of lover boy's horse heading for his moment of pleasure. The soldier stopped for a moment to see if the washing was hanging out, before continuing on his way. Olly believed that to be a signal to say he was out, because just after he'd supposedly headed off to market, he'd watched as his wife hung out his dirty clothes that he knew she hadn't yet washed.

'Anyway, he left them to it, waiting and waiting, the anger building up and raging inside him as he thought of the antics that were taking place under his roof. Eventually soldier boy came trotting back up the track, so Olly stepped out from the bushes in front of him and discharged a bolt from his crossbow deep into his chest, just below the heart. The soldier fell to the ground, squealing like a pig, so Olly finished him off with his hammer.

'The crossbow is Olly's weapon of choice around here, followed quickly with the hammer to stifle the animal's groans. He saw no reason not to use the same means on lover boy too, and it worked well. No guns used around here, not with the garrison just down the road. It goes without saying, doesn't it?'

Olly climbed from his chair and walked over to the window area that Dick had vacated earlier. He stared across the wet, sodden marshes. 'It's strange,' he said, 'but every morning when I rise, I look across these low wetlands and see a kestrel hovering over the very spot where I buried the bastard. It's as if the rodents are drawn to the smell of his decomposing body and the kestrel is drawn there because of the rodents. Interesting, don't you think?'

Olly turned from the window and placed himself back down in his favourite chair, adding, 'I buried him whilst he was still warm, then I came home late, as expected, and climbed into bed with her like nothing had happened. She asked me how I was, and I told her I'd had a murderous day, but was fine now I was home.'

James spluttered and coughed, almost choking on his ale as it mistakenly made its way into his windpipe because of his laughing. 'There's that dry black humour again. No wonder you get on so well with Jerry,' he said.

James directed his gaze to the kitchen window, instantly realising the impact of his thoughtless sobering words. 'Sorry,' he added. 'I still keep thinking he's with us.' His eyes moistened, blurring his vision. 'Wishful thinking, heh?'

'What about the horse? It was a military horse, so it would be instantly recognisable,' said Dick in an attempt to draw the conversation back on track.

Olly slowly lifted his feet as if they were made of lead and plonked them down heavily on to his footstall, whilst scratching the back of his head. 'The pigs,' he said in a lazy drawl.

'The pigs?' asked Dick.

'Aye, they can't live on fresh air, you know. Money's tight.'

James chuckled yet again. 'Two birds with one stone, heh Olly?' he said.

Olly's face erupted into a broad creepy grin. 'Exactly, cousin, exactly. Two birdies with one stone!'

The room momentarily fell silent as they sipped their ales. Olly took a deep breath before continuing. 'That's not the end of it though. A week later she was all but climbing the bloody walls, going out of her skull she was, wondering where on earth her fresh-faced soldier boy had got to. He obviously hadn't told anyone at the garrison of his little exploits with my missus, and they thought he must have done a bunk. A month later I told her I didn't want her around anymore because she was so bloody miserable, and I sent her back to her mother's. So, there you have it…me and my wife are history.'

Kennington Common
3 September 1795

THE BODY of Jerry Avershaw still hung in its gibbet cage. No movement, no dignity and for the first time no guards. That predictable day had finally arrived when the powers that be let it be known that enough was enough. The days had turned into weeks, the loose whispers gathering their momentum like a snowball tumbling down a hill – the highwayman's body was now alone.

The thieves and vagabonds from all around moved in like small clans of hyenas, their low-born opportunistic natures entwined with distorted sentiment, concluding in a strange pilgrimage to his gibbet during the hours of darkness, whereupon they procured from his decaying body the bones of his fingers and toes to convert into stoppers for their tobacco pipes.

The tyro villains contented themselves with tearing the buttons from his rotting clothes as mementos of the estimation in which they held their arch prototype. As night merged into day, the vile twisted creatures returned to their lowly hovels, chuffed beyond words with the proceeds of their night's gruesome endeavours.

******

One week later, two of the thieves were confronted by three men on horses, the brims of their hats pulled down over their eyes, their masks raised.

'Damn your eyes, stop, you fuckers!' growled one of the highwaymen, as they encircled the two unkempt men, who looked more than capable of handing out what they were about to receive had the boot been on the other foot.

'You won't find anything here, my friends, we're of the same like as yourselves,' said one of the two men through yellow, cankered teeth.

'You're no friend of ours, and you're not of our fucking like!' The same highwayman stormed. 'Now dismount from those nags slowly, very fucking slowly, and remove your boots. Come now gents, do you really think we're foolish enough to hide our valuables in our boots like some cocooned aristocrat?'

'Remove your fucking boots. Now!' demanded the lead highwayman.

The men removed their boots with the wearisome reluctance of a sloth. The three highwaymen jumped from their horses, with pistols trained on the now barefoot men. They bound them back to back and sat them down. Their pockets were searched.

'What have we here then?' quizzed one of the high tobys, as he dangled a pouch under the nose of one of the men.

'It's only a tobacco pouch, just a tobacco pouch,' replied the man.

The high toby wasn't convinced. 'What's with the button attached to its tie?' he asked.

'It's just a family thing, a bit of sentiment, that's all,' the man replied. 'So, I'd appreciate it if you didn't relieve me of such a small insignificant thing that's of no value to you.' The high toby continued with his search, delving deep into the man's other pocket. He glared angrily at his find, and an uncomfortable silence momentarily ensued as the atmosphere rapidly turned for the worse. 'What's this?' he asked the man.

'It's only my pipe,' came the nervous reply.

'No, fucker, I'll ask you again. What's this?' The highwayman held the pipe under the man's nose, tapping its stopper with his finger. The man began to sweat and shiver uncontrollably. His friend's emotions also ran the same path, as he witnessed the incriminating discovery of their previous week's work unfold.

'Here's another pipe,' one of the other highwaymen said. 'This fucker's got one as well, with an identical bone stopper, and his tobacco pouch carries an identical button. Either they both have a sentimental family thing going on or they're a pair of liars.'

'Stand them up,' barked the lead highwayman, his angry words receiving instant response. 'Gag them with their own stinking socks!'

One of the other highwaymen picked up one of the men's rancid socks and hesitated for a moment before walking around to the other bound man.

'We can't have you chewing on your own socks now, can we,' he said. 'Seeing you boys like to share things so much, you can share each other's.'

The highwaymen laughed as they watched the two men's discomfort, before turning off the laughter in an instant. One of the highwaymen reached into his pocket and retrieved a surgeon's scalpel. The men's screams were muffled, and their blood flowed freely. Their contempt for the dead had come at a price.

The Oxford Arms, Warwick Lane, London
12 September 1795

WOLF WINTERMAN sat in the corner of the bar with his brother. He'd only minutes earlier turned the key in the lock of his beloved brandy shop door. Business was over for another day.

'Well, well. Oi oi, look who's 'ere,' said Wolf aloud, as three men swaggered through the door towards them. Wolf waved an arm towards the barmaid, signalling with his fingers for three more ales. 'Well, did ya catch up with 'em?' Wolf asked the new arrivals.

James removed two tobacco pouches from his pocket, opening them and pouring their contents on to the table. Wolf grimaced in horror as he turned towards his brother. 'What's this, an eye for an eye or something?' he remarked. Olly's eyes narrowed to mere slits as he spoke through tightened lips. 'A toe for a toe, more like. It's something that had to be done.'

'Is that a fucking thumb?' Squealed Wolf, as he distanced himself from the table, pointing in revulsion.

'Fingers and thumbs, fingers and toes. It's alright, don't you go worrying yourself none, they're still alive and kicking,' replied Olly.

James laughed. 'Well they would be if they had any of their toes.'

Wolf looked at them despondently. 'I don't know if that's a good thing or not, boys,' he said.

'What do you mean?' asked James.

'If they're still alive, albeit missing a few things here and there, they're not going to be very happy,' explained Wolf. 'That means more enemies made, boys, so you can't stay around here for too long. If these people don't have the enthusiasm to come back at you themselves, they'll most probably go to the authorities and try to seek revenge that way. Did they recognise any of ya?'

'Nah, we were masked,' said Dick.

'Well, they'll soon put one and one together if they haven't already and put you and James in the picture. Olly's the only one who's not going to be looked upon as a suspect,' said Wolf. He straightened himself in his chair, resuming his composure before adding, 'Jesus, I didn't want to bring this up at this moment in time but sometimes you have to make allowances.' He inhaled deeply. 'I paid some old lags to cut down Jerry. I knew it would be too risky for you boys to cut him down and, besides, you weren't around, so I took it upon myself to get the job done and restore some dignity back to our friend.

'My brother Wade will take you to him when you feel the time is right to lay him to rest. I've had his body wrapped in linen with plenty of lavender. Prepare yourself boys, cos the old lags told me there isn't much left of him, especially after the other day when a battalion of soldiers passed by his gibbet and decided to use him as target practice. There was quite a bit of uproar about it because some members of the public witnessed their vindictive behaviour and reported it, but you can rest assured it will fall on deaf ears. That's when I decided to get things done and get him away from there. It didn't come cheap, expecting people to risk their lives over a dead man, but Jerry was a good friend, so it was the least I could do for him.'

'It will return to you in other ways Wolf, we'll make sure of that,' said Dick, as he watched James instantly recoil into himself, too overcome to speak.

Wolf nodded in appreciation. 'There'll be no need for that. I'd feel offended if you did,' he said. 'Some things in life have priority over money and this is one such occasion. By the way, what did you say to these scamps before you set about them with your amateur surgery?'

Olly smiled and said, 'I just asked them if they really believed their actions to be respectful, and did they really think they had Jerry's memory at heart.'

Wolf nodded whilst pursing his lips. 'Interesting, interesting,' he replied.

The Queen's Head, Stanmore, London
4 September 1795

'I HAVE a farm to look after, and it's time I put myself back there. All this flitting back and forth is taking its toll on my senses, not to mention my aching bones,' Olly said to James and Dick.

James gave a half-suppressed, derisory grin. 'Ooh, the death clock's ticking for galloping Dick Ferguson and James Myers, and when death comes to town it's best not to be around,' he replied sarcastically.

Olly looked at James and mirrored the same snarky smile, saying, 'You know sure as hell that isn't the reason and I never once said I was going to give up my farm. It has to be said, I'm not wanted by the authorities. I know I should be, but I'm not, and I have all intentions of keeping it that way. That said, the door of my home will always be open to the pair of you, whenever you need it, for as long as need be. When I return home, the first thing I'm going to do is feed my animals, and the second thing I'm going to do is lay some floorboards between the rafters in the roof, enough room for you both to lay your heads.'

The two outlaws gave an appreciative smile. 'Will you at least stay and have some supper with us before you head back, cousin?' asked James.

Olly smiled back, replying, 'That I will. Is that pork I smell?'

The Bowl and Kettle Inn, Edgware, London 16 September 1795

'I'VE SEEN one of those men before,' whispered Dick Ferguson, as he watched two men pass by their table, port in hand.

'Where was that?' asked James as he weighed the two men up, both physically and psychologically.

'I'm not sure, but I think it was when I worked for the hackney carriage company,' Dick replied. After a few seconds it came to him. 'White's…yes, it was White's. That's where I saw him. He frequents White's Gentlemen's Club in St James's. Pompous arrogant bastard, the type that swayed me into thinking the hassle that came with the job didn't justify its wages. Never short of a flippant remark that one.'

'Well, Dicky boy, he doesn't recognise you, does he?' said James, his face breaking into a sinister grin, as his eyes followed the men's every move. Meanwhile, the two men were totally unaware of the undivided attention being lavished upon them.

'No, the little bleeder doesn't recognise you at all.' James added, chuckling. 'These dainty boys are in for the night. They won't be leaving here until the morning. I think they deserve an early morning surprise, what say you Dick?'

'I think so, my friend. I think we have a debt to Olly that has to be repaid sooner rather than later.'

Police Office, Union Hall
17 September 1795, 4 pm

'YES, CORPORAL Boare, please make it quick, I have a raging headache,' moaned John Townsend, as he removed his coat and planted himself down solemnly at his desk.

'We've just been informed of a highway robbery in Edgware. My instincts tell me it might be of interest to you,' reported the corporal.

'Please carry on, Corporal, and pour me a brandy while you tell me,' replied Townsend, handing the key of his tantalus decanter to his officer.

'Well, guv, a Sergeant Williams has filed a report of a failed highway robbery that he was witness to, of two gents who reside on our manor.'

'Failed you say?' enquired Townsend.

'Yes, guv,' said the corporal as he handed Townsend his brandy. 'The two chaps were being held up at gunpoint when they were distracted upon the appearance of Sergeant Williams, who came across them by chance. The sergeant fired a ball at them without hesitation but missed and they took off. Both were on geldings, one a bay and the other a dun. They didn't attempt to return fire. They seemed to know they could easily outride him, and that they did.

But here's the intriguing part. As the chase neared its end and Sergeant Williams, in his words not mine, gave up knackered, one of the rogues reined in his horse and turned towards him, lifting his hat and arrogantly giving him what he described as a cheeky royal wave, before turning and galloping off after his accomplice. I asked him which horse the scoundrel was on and he told me it was the bay. Doesn't that remind you of someone who made an appearance at this very window not so long ago?'

'It certainly sounds like our man and one of his cronies.' agreed Townsend. 'I think it's time to come out all guns blazing, Corporal, and hunt these deplorable characters down to put an end to their activities, because as sure as eggs are eggs, they'll not stop until they're apprehended. They've reached that fearful point of no return. Their circumstances have changed considerably, and they know it. It's only a matter of time…weeks, months maybe, even the odd year or so may pass…but their theatre of operation is shrinking. They're like fish in a pond during a never-ending drought. Time isn't on their side. Their day of reckoning will come, you mark my words, Corporal.'

Penal Colony, Port Jackson,
New South Wales, Australia
28 November 1795

MATHEW CAPLIN continued unloading bricks from the cart as he watched the newly arrived convicts make their way ashore, discreetly glancing over every so often as he worked, not wishing to antagonise his guards and overseers. He'd made good progress since his arrival and was now in good standing with the men who held total control over the quality of his existence, and he intended to keep it that way.

The sun was setting, and another hard day's graft was finally drawing to its end. He and his friend Bill Chandler, who had been sentenced alongside him, returned with the rest of the transportees to their small wooden huts behind the stockade, where Caplin slumped, exhausted into his hammock. Rest was everything to survival of the following day's onslaught of hard labour. As he lay back, sweat slowly trickled down his sun-blistered forehead in small beads, which made their way into his tired eyes, causing them to sting.

'Mathew!' barked a young thin-faced overseer. 'A guard from one of the new arrivals has asked me to give you this letter. It must be of some importance because he paid me for the privilege. 'I thought you wrong 'uns were supposed to run around for me, not the other way around?'

Mathew Caplin forced a smile at the overseer's light-hearted banter. 'Thank you, sir,' he replied as he took the letter from the overseer with his work-beaten, heavily calloused hand, and placed himself down on to a stool to read its contents. His excitement turned quickly to anger as he found his fingers and thumbs too swollen to carry out the trivial task of opening it.

'Bill, open this letter for me,' he called begrudgingly to his friend across the hut. 'The swelling in my fingers is making it nigh-on impossible to open the bloody thing.' Bill Chandler took the letter from his agitated friend and fumbled with it for what seemed like a lifetime, before handing it back to him with a smile of accomplishment.

'Looks to me like your hands are a close second to mine, Billy boy,' said Caplin, making light of their painfully unpleasant predicament.

'Tell me about it. God only knows how we're going to get through tomorrow,' said Bill with a disheartened whine. 'Listen to me,' replied Caplin. 'We'll get through every day until our time is done. The bastards who put us here have done so to try to break us. Are you going to give them the pleasure of knowing they've done just that, or are you going to finish your sentence standing tall and saying fuck the lot of you!'

Bill looked at Caplin, eyebrows raised, before saying, 'You could always lift my spirits, Mathew, no matter what the situation. You have such a gift with words.' Bill grinned broadly, adding, 'Aye, fuck the lot of them. They're not going to break us.'

Mathew Caplin settled down to read his letter, studying it carefully as if hanging on its every word.

'Well, what does it say?' asked Bill. 'Come on, put me out of my misery.'

Caplin read from the letter: 'It says, it is with deep regret that we the empowered have to inform you that your close friend Miss Catherine Jane Forster, who was under your keep at the Marshalsea prison, Southwark, Surrey, had taken it upon herself to abscond, and whilst doing so was murdered outside a butchery on Borough High Street of the same parish. The cause of death was from a deep horizontal laceration to the throat, thought to be inflicted by a very sharp knife or quite possibly a shaving razor. The letter is dated five months ago, and she met her death the week before.'

Caplin smirked with deep satisfaction as he passed the letter to his friend, who knowingly returned a grin back to him. 'The elimination of the woman responsible for our public humiliation and incarceration in this foreign land has been successful, Billy boy. Now our bitter battle with the torturous years ahead will be just that little bit easier to contend with, for what we schemed and followed through with such grand success is worth a cart ride to the gallows. We, my friend, have just literally got away with murder, but let's not forget our friend Avershaw, let's hope he also gets his comeuppance.'

'What better motivator could you wish for to keep you going through this living hell than good old-fashioned revenge?' Bill replied, as he looked over the letter once more, tittering to himself.

'What's so funny, Billy boy?' asked Caplin.

'Outside the butchery. She met her end outside the butchery. Very creative, don't you think?'

Penal Colony, Port Jackson, New South Wales 20 January 1796

MATHEW CAPLIN stared at his reflection in the mirror, studying his weather-beaten face, which showed wrinkles. He pawed at the deep creases that entrenched his skin and belied his true years. Working outside in the midday sun, day in and day out had taken its toll. His muscular bronzed arms, however, told a different story, for they wouldn't have looked amiss on a well-conditioned man several years his junior.

He walked over towards a bucket that was resting on a makeshift table in the corner of the room and placed both his hands simultaneously into it, scooping out the contents and splashing it over his hot sunburned forehead. The cold water felt good, even a little calming.

More convict ships had moored in the bay that morning. It was a thing he'd grown to look forward to. There would always be some new arrival who could string a half-decent sentence together and be more than willing to share the goings-on back home in old England with him. Occasionally, his lurid past would travel full circle and catch up with him, resulting in him crossing paths with an individual who had fallen foul of his distorted ways and harboured a bitter grudge towards him. But it didn't bother him none. He was far too thick-skinned and well established with the guards to concern himself with the odd undernourished, dishevelled minion who had just set foot on these alien shores.

His moment of solitude was interrupted by a call from one of the guards, who had taken a shine to Caplin's intellectual, upper-class humour that he could turn on at the drop of a hat.

'I have a letter from England for you, Mathew. It was handed to me by one of the crew who arrived this morning.'

'Thank you kindly,' replied Caplin.

'I'll read it later, once I've washed,' he told the noticeably disheartened messenger, who was hoping to be given the opportunity to share its contents.

Caplin waited until the guard closed the door after him before setting about opening the piece of communication that had travelled so far without gaining unwanted attention.

My dear friend Mathew,

I hope you are keeping well! I am told the conditions are harsh to say the least, and the avoidance of disease is likened to a roll of the dice. But I am sure if anyone can rise above the hardships incurred under such ferocious circumstances, it is your good self.

I am writing this letter with some expectance that it may never reach your hands. But one must undoubtedly give it one's best shot. After all, half a chance is better than none, don't you think?

I tried in vain to track down the messenger of my last letter to you, but alas I discovered he passed away from the wretched typhoid. So, I have been placed in the awful predicament of taking my chances with somebody else.

Fortunately, I have managed to procure the ship's religious instructor. I think it safe to say it is better I place my trust in him rather than some heathen who is overzealous with the lash.

Please forgive me for being so brief, but I have to keep what I am going to say to the bare minimum, for I am aware this letter could quite easily fall into the wrong hands, so I will come straight to the point of why I am writing to you.

Lewis Jeremiah Avershaw was tried and sentenced to the penalty of death on 30 July 1795 at Croydon Assizes, for the murder of Bow Street Runner David Price and the attempted murder of fellow Runners Bernard Turner and Barnaby Windsor at the Three Brewers Public House in Maid Lane, Southwark. He was hung on Kennington Common on 3 August 1795, and also received the post-death indignity of being gibbeted at Putney Bottom, the scene of several of his crimes. His close friend and fellow criminal Henry Watts was sentenced to death at the same Croydon Assizes shortly afterwards for the highway robbery of three captains of the militia, was hung on Wimbledon Common and gibbeted at the exact location of where his crime took place. His body was later stolen away by persons unknown.

The remaining fragments of the gang are either imprisoned or on the run. I hope I am the bearer of news that has raised your spirits somewhat and given you food for thought as to the direction to which you will take your life in the future after your release, when that wonderful time comes, and it will!

I will continue to take care of your ongoing business affairs, so upon your release you can make your decision on what you wish to do. Stay strong my friend.

Your trusted friend,
Edwin E. Clarke

Mathew Caplin called and beckoned his trusted friend Bill Chandler. 'What is it?' Chandler asked, his eyes drawn to the letter clutched in Caplin's hand.

'Read this,' Caplin whispered smugly. Bill Chandler ran his eyes over the letter swiftly, his smile of satisfaction broadening with every sentence he absorbed.

'That's going to save us a lot of bother, innit?' said Chandler. 'Although I must admit, it doesn't come as a great surprise. Ill fame carries many a burden, and one of them is a short life span.'

Caplin returned to his mirror, running his fingers over his wrinkled brown skin. 'It does indeed, Billy boy, it does indeed. Do you know something? That little piece of paper sitting precariously on the edge of that table is a total game changer. It is of such significance that it's probably the single biggest influence in the whole of my life.'

Bill Chandler looked at his friend, who was still transfixed on the mirror in front of him. 'That big, huh?' Chandler said.

'Yes, that big,' Caplin replied. 'It's just told me I don't have to return to damp old England and give myself another bloody cough. And as for my consistent nightly dreams of chasing high tobys around every spinney and turnpike…I think I can safely say they've been permanently laid to rest. As from this moment in time, they're history. I may just as well live out the rest of my days in this beautiful land. Yes! When the time comes for the powers that be to tell me to collect up my belongings and go and better myself, that's exactly what I'm going to do.'

Bill Chandler cracked a smile along with a chuckle. 'Aye, aye, me old mate. Me too, me too,' he said.

CPSIA information can be obtained
at www.ICGtesting.com
Printed in the USA
LVHW041502290322
714698LV00010B/375

9 781398 430983